THE ENTREI
MARKETIN
SYSTEM

The **Proven Step-by-Step System** to
Getting All The Customers You'll Ever Need...

...Rhythmically & Consistently – like clockwork.

NIGEL BOTTERILL

⊘EntrepreneursCircle

Published in 2021 by Entrepreneurs Circle Ltd

A catalogue number for this book is available from the British Library
ISBN 978-1-5272-8369-5

Entrepreneurs Circle Ltd, Reg No: 07484456

This is a work of non-fiction.

In some cases the names and identifying characteristics of individuals have been
changed to protect their privacy.

Printed and bound in Great Britain by Eazyprint, Northants.

For all the entrepreneurs and small business owners out there who work so hard, often without recognition, to provide the jobs, pay the taxes, fuel the economy and keep the world spinning.

We salute you.

Contents

Introduction:

The Entrepreneur's Marketing and Sales System is a system that's taken over 10 years to hone, refine and test.

There's been a lot of trial, error and testing to come up with what is now a very robust means for any business to crack the rhythmic acquisition of customers.

You'll need to have a deep understanding of the whole System if you're going to use it in your business.

It's taken the best part of 25 years for us to learn this stuff – and 10 years to put the System together. But now it's here you can deploy it to crack the 'holy grail' for any business; the rhythmic acquisition of customers.

I hope it all makes sense – and that you enjoy it.

Most importantly, I know you'll find it useful...

January 2021

P.S - you can download the accompanying poster of the EMS System at: **https://EMSSystem.co.uk/poster**

It will help you visualise what we reference throughout this book and is perfect to stick on your office walls too.

CHAPTER ONE:
THE PYRAMID

"It always seems impossible until it's done"

Nelson Mandela

Every business fits somewhere in this pyramid. ⟶

At the top of the pyramid, are the 1% of business owners that are seriously rich;

Next are the 4% of business owners who are doing great;

The third *'slice'* are the 15% who are getting there. They're earning a good living.

Next is the biggest chunk: 60% of all businesses are *'getting by'*. They're bobbing along. Surviving – but not thriving. Paying their bills – just.

There's always a challenge of some sort for these business owners – whether it's clearing the VAT bill this month, meeting payroll or taking on another credit card. These are all symptoms of people in the 60%.

Then at the bottom of the pyramid, there are 20% of business owners who at any one time, are broke.

Now, obviously, you want to move up the pyramid towards the top. That's where you want to be, right?

On that basis then, you've got to start paying attention to the people at the top of the pyramid.

This is an obvious and easy thing to say, but what we've discovered over the years is that it's actually quite a difficult thing to do in practice.

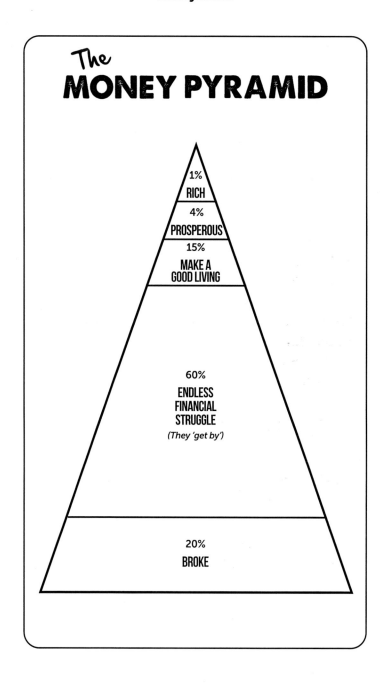

Let's face it, **knowing something is very different to actually doing it.**

What I'm hoping will happen though, is that you'll read this book, take that knowledge and start to do it.

It's the execution and implementation of what you know that makes the difference.

It's your behaviours – not your knowledge - that actually moves you up the pyramid.

It's not about knowing the stuff; it's about doing the stuff.

And, if you pay attention, drill down and closely observe individuals and people that you know are towards the top of the pyramid, you'll find that they do the stuff that you know about, but aren't doing.

Sounds really easy. But it's not.

It's difficult to change behaviour and change thinking.

But that's what we're going to do.

I need you to recognise that the reason why this System is so important – the reason why cracking the rhythmic acquisition of customers is so critical to your future – is because it moves you up this pyramid.

It takes you from perpetual financial struggle to a place where you can actually have a really lovely life.

Now there are plenty of people, us included, who've made the journey.

I didn't start at the top of the pyramid.

I've moved up the pyramid.

And I started by fundamentally doing two things:

   1. I paid attention and learned the right things
   2. Then I rigorously executed and implemented...

and it's that execution and implementation that made the difference.

This is *really* significant.

This is not a book about you learning more interesting stuff *(although you will!)*.

This is a book about equipping you to execute better, more effectively, and more successfully.

Most entrepreneurs don't own a business, they own a job.

Think about it. They've become a slave to their business, walking around dragging a ball and chain with them.

They started out of passion, pursuing freedom, and a hunger for more, but somewhere along the journey they lost their way.

(Losing your way begins with you checking your email as soon as your eyes open in the morning – it's a really dumb thing to do because it means you're letting other people set the agenda for your day, decide what you think about and focus on. People at the top of the pyramid don't do that.)

Most business owners *(the ones in the 60% and the 20%)* get bogged down in the weeds. They languish in the tactical hell of dealing with time-sucking activities that drain the life out of them and don't move their business forward.

You will know the extent to which this applies to you.

Be aware. Because what I've just described are behaviours of the 60% and 20%.

And the 60% and the 20% are not at the top of pyramid.

Now compare that with an entrepreneur who owns a thriving business that's wildly successful.

A business that consistently generates leads, clients and revenue every week like clockwork.

The business owner has automated systems and a team in place to run the daily operation and take care of the grunt work of the business.

They command higher prices and make more profit.
They're growing fast.

The Pyramid

What's the difference between one chef who started a catering business and 20 years later realised that he has created a job *(not a business)* and another who started a catering business and 10 years later has 16 locations and then sells it for a multi-million pound payout?

The difference isn't in their abilities as a chef. Or in the food.

The difference is in what each chef thought about and focused on. And what they did; the actions they took.

Those actions were all about the marketing and the selling of the food.

This applies to your business too.

Now, I know that you know that. I know that's not a revelation.

But it's still a behaviour that's not reflected by enough people.

It's one of the reasons why people are stuck down the bottom end of the pyramid; because they think about – and focus on – the wrong things.

The single most important rule in any business is that, as the owner, your number one responsibility is to get and keep enough customers.

Think about it, your entire existence as an entrepreneur lives and dies by how effective you are at producing revenue.

What happens to you next year is going to be determined by how effective you are at producing new revenue.

If you've got a marketing and sales machine that predictably brings in new customers every day like clockwork, owning a business can be phenomenal.

If you don't, it can be unpredictable and highly stressful.

This is because the destiny of your company, your income, and the income of your employees rest on whatever fate drops in your lap.

We all know people like that.

Now you can choose to ignore it and turn a blind eye, or you can make the shift and join the winning side by installing a marketing and selling system in your business.

That's what this book will help you to do.

Either way, you must understand that all the latest, shiny marketing tactics, hacks, and tools won't solve the number one problem around how to get more customers. They tackle the symptom, but not the cause.

More tactics are not the answer, and deep down you probably already know that.

If you're like most business owners, you've gone through all the different CRM systems, landing-page builders and all the funnels, and you've found that it hasn't actually moved you meaningfully forward. That's because all these tactics are designed to treat the symptoms of low sales, and not cure the symptomatic cause of the problem.

You need a system – a system that will bring you consistent leads, enquiries and buyers.

Over the next two to three years, we're going to see the era of the professional business person.

What that means is we're going to see people who are professional at properly running their businesses.

It's not about being professional at what you do *(although that is important)*.

There are plenty of accountants who are amateurs at actually building an accountancy practice but very professional at being an accountant.

What we're talking about here is the era of the professional business person who's able to manage and run their business in a professional, proper way. And, right at the core of that is cracking the rhythmic acquisition of customers.

The businesses that crack this – and the business owners who start to live and breathe this – are the ones that will flourish and succeed in the coming years.

Moreover, part of being a professional business person means that you've cracked the rhythmic acquisition of customers.

You've put in place the system that delivers you the enquiries and leads that you need to increase the revenue so that you've got the money to deliver the right level of service that provides the value that you want to provide to your customers.

(Read that last paragraph again – its important!)

All of those things require cash, and the cash comes from the rhythmic acquisition of customers.

The professional business person is someone who EXECUTES what he/she knows.

The professional business person isn't content just to know something and not do it.

The professional business person recognises the worthlessness of knowing something and not doing it.

One of the ways that you can make the leap towards becoming a professional business person is to get yourself out of the weeds.

The weeds are the stuff that wraps and ultimately tangles you up.

It's all the day-to-day stuff that has to be dealt with in the business. But if the business owner spends his/her time dealing with all these tasks, it can be absolutely fatal to any progression up the pyramid.

If you're doing lots of day-to-day *'grunt work'* in your business then you're screwed. You need the mental and physical capacity to move yourself up the pyramid.

Without it you'll be languishing pretty much where you are right now. Only you know if that's a problem or not.

For example, if you're a dentist and you spend all your working hours in your surgery drilling, you're not a professional business person. You may be a wonderfully accomplished dentist but your practice will not move very far forward in the next 12 months because you're stuck in the weeds.

Now we all have to do some of the grunt work, we recognise that. But we have to get out of the weeds every week for a decent chunk of time. The extent to which we're able to get out of those weeds will be a big factor in how far we get.

Because you can't implement this system if you're stuck in the weeds.

When I first started the Entrepreneurs Circle, I talked a lot about the power of 90 minutes. I even wrote a very successful book called 'Build your business in 90 minutes a day'!

Logically and intellectually everybody gets it. They understand the impact of spending 90 minutes focusing on the things that will make your business more successful.

But the number of people who actually do it on a daily basis is really tiny.

People think that I just talk about it and that I don't actually do it. They're wrong.

One of the big leaps that I've made over the last 18 months is that I have no responsibilities in my business. Beyond looking after my Mastermind group and Inner Circle coaching clients, I have nothing else to do.

There's somebody else who's responsible for everything else.

This liberates me!

Now I've got up to 25 hours a week to do the stuff that will move my business forward.

I'm well out of the weeds. And we need to get you there too!

To do that, those 90 minutes become really important. The things we're going to cover are impossible to implement without it.

Here's a little exercise. Humour me and try it out:

Just imagine that you've acquired your business today. You've just bought it.

Today is day one. You're the investor who's put up the cash to fund the purchase.

What are you going to do?

How would an investor look at your business?
What would they think?

Their perspective will be markedly different because investors are only concerned, broadly speaking, with the return they can get on their investment.

So, if they've invested capital, an investor is interested in getting a return on it.

What numbers would they look at?

What would their expectations be for next year?

What would their view be of the management? And the staff?

An investor's job isn't to keep you busy for five or six *(or even seven!)* days a week. That's not the aim of the investor, and it wasn't your aim either when you set out on day one (*we'll reconnect you with your goals and your dreams from your real 'Day One' shortly*).

Thinking and looking at your business like an investor can be a really smart thing to do.

And a professional business person would think about their business just like an investor would think about it.

Most business owners' efforts aren't organised around any kind of system, philosophy, or plan.

Most people will look at the week or the day ahead and then deal with it by reacting.

The system that we're going to give you provides an opportunity for you to organise your efforts.

Most people go to work and then do what's urgent today.

When you do what's urgent today, it means you're continually responding to other people's agendas and to what other people have messaged or emailed you. It's a sure-fire way to keep you pegged down in the bottom half of the pyramid.

It makes it very difficult for you to put in place any kind of system when your time is fragmented.

Somehow, some way, you need a system that will enable you to organise your efforts.

Meet Celia Gaze...

She's had tremendous success in recent years with her business up in the North West of England. She adopted quite an extreme approach because she goes and checks into a hotel every other week.

She books in for one night and chooses her hotel carefully. The room has to have two beds. One to sleep in; one to work on. She doesn't want a hotel that's got any kind of facilities, because that will be tempting for her. She can't have a gym or a pool *(and if the bar's really shitty that's a good thing too)* because she's there to work.

She spreads out all her work, locks herself in her room, and doesn't leave the hotel until she's got it done. That's how she executes. A little dramatic or extreme? Maybe. But devastatingly effective? For sure.

And Celia's income has soared since she started doing this. She rocketed up that pyramid.

We all have to trick ourselves sometimes.

No one is pretending this is easy.

It's obvious and logical, but it isn't easy because we're human beings and we're very fallible.

We're very good at procrastinating. But somehow, some way, you need a system that enables you to do the things that need to be done.

You can start by creating some time this week.

It's just like getting fit or losing weight. If you eat the right food this week, your body will start to change. But if you go back and revert to the same food you ate last week, it will revert again.

It's just like that in business.

We need a system to organise our time. A system that will help you understand what to say yes or no to because you've now got a point of reference.

Professional business people understand that controlling their time, and effectively managing it, is the single biggest enabler to everything else that needs to happen.

They recognise that and they go through the pain barrier of ensuring that what it takes to make it work happens.

For some of you, your workplace will be stacked against you in this regard.

You'll work in an office that you share with other people. You'll have nowhere that you can go where you can shut the door and just focus.

If that's you, then you need to find somewhere that you can go. You might have to get a little bit creative, but you need to be away from the distractions of the world.

Working at home can sometimes work really well *(as long as the house is empty and there's no one coming in)*. If you've got an office door that you can shut and you can't hear what's happening outside, it can be great.

You'll not make this System happen without the right environment and organisation of your time and your space. This System can and will make the rhythmic acquisition of customers a reality for you.

It's possible that there may be an exception, a business that's in some way so specific and unique and different that this system doesn't apply, but it's probably not yours!

Transforming a business from where it is now to where you want it to be – to move it markedly up that pyramid – is not about doing a thousand different things. It's about finding one big thing at a time and leveraging that.

One of the elements that this System is definitely going to help you with is knowing exactly what you need to focus on tomorrow.

The Pyramid

It won't be ten things. It'll be one thing.

Then, when you get that done, there'll be another thing.

And then there'll be another, and there'll be another...

The System gives you an order and a structure to do it. Feeling overwhelmed will disappear.

A little word of warning though: the System is not à la carte.

For the System to work, you can't pick and choose.

Some of the elements you'll warm to and be naturally keener about than others. But you have to do the ones that are difficult and that you don't like.

If you start to skip bits in the System, you'll have rigged the System.

Don't skip bits. Please. You'll ruin it for yourself – and the price you'll pay will be languishing in the pyramid.

That pyramid's important.

Decide where you want to be on it.
Then *(honestly)* evaluate where you are right now.

The Entrepreneurs Marketing and Sales System can take you from where you are now on the pyramid to where you want to be.

Providing you follow the system...

CHAPTER TWO:
THE WEEDS

"If you tend to a flower it will bloom, no matter how many weeds surround it"

Matshona Dhliwayo

In this chapter, we're going to explain the System and begin the implementation process.

Brace yourself!

In simple terms, there are five parts to the system.

The first part is understanding your gap. The gap between where you are now and where you want to be.

If there isn't a gap, you don't need the System.

If your business is fine and dandy and delivering what you want it to deliver, you're making the money you want to earn and the customers are coming in, you don't need the System.

If it ain't broke, don't fix it.

But seen as how you're still reading we figure you've probably got a gap. And it might be quite a big one.

Well, worry not. The first part of the System is to properly understand what your gap is.

Where do you want to be?

Once you're clear on your gap, the System moves into arguably the most important part – your Foundation Blocks.

There are 11 Foundation Blocks and if you skip any of them the impact will be like a wheel falling off your car.

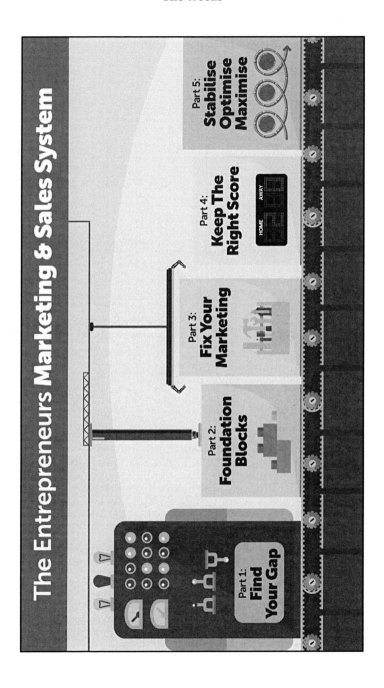

You've got to get your Foundation Blocks right.

Once we get your Foundation Blocks sorted, Part Three of the System *(Fixing Your Marketing)* is easy.

What's your market?

What's your utterly compelling message for your market?

And what's the best media to take your message to your market?

Simples.

Next, the bit that makes the System work – the magic bit*(!)* – is Part Four *(Knowing the Score)*.

In sport, if you don't know the score, you don't know who's winning or who's losing. Well that applies to marketing as well.

In the era of the professional business person, it's tracking the right numbers, and doing the right things with them, that keeps the System on target to close your gap.

You'll love Part Four because it helps you see your progress up the pyramid. Without it you'll be lost.

Part Five is not really a part, rather it seeks to recognise that the System will never be complete.

It really is like the painting of the Forth Bridge. We looked this up and it's true: they've never stopped painting it. When they reach one end, they have to start again. They're continuously painting.

And so it is with the Entrepreneurs Marketing and Sales System - it never gets done.

There are three 'cycles' around the System.

During the first cycle, we're going to stabilise everything. We're going to put the right stuff in place and we're going to do it broadly, but competently. This first cycle will typically take six to nine months minimum to execute properly. But the prize is magnificent and so worthwhile to your elevation up the pyramid.

Second time round, we'll optimise the System.
Ordinarily this takes another nine to twelve months but by then, your position in the top echelons of the pyramid will be secure.

When we're finished optimising, we go around it all again and maximise it.

There'll always be ways that we can do things better.

Now, if we start to try and optimise it the first time round, the System takes a lot longer. The results become a lot slower. That's why we stabilise first and then optimise.

It's a system that will keep moving. We can always optimise and make every little element or Foundation Block better. We'll be able to optimise every piece of marketing and make it better.

And when you optimise after you've stabilised, you end up with a very different result.

This System can fundamentally do two big things for business owners.

- It can crack the rhythmic acquisition of customers *(which is the holy grail for everyone in business)* and, in most businesses...

- ...it can also give you, as a business owner, a pay rise every other month.

We put that out there because in the era of the professional business person, a professional business person will recognise that the profitability of his/her business is a really important thing.

That's what gives you the money for the stuff that you want to do – both in your business and in your personal life.

As part of that, your pay becomes a really key measure.

Lots of people in business have become good at not paying themselves very much.

They're amateur business owners and we're in the era of the professional business owner.

Professional business owners always pay themselves properly.

There are some people who are working in their business for less than the minimum wage. Guess where they are on the pyramid?

When we work out the hours that you put in, look at the money that you take out and we compute it, it's not legal what some of these folk are doing to themselves but it's another symptom of being down the bottom end of the pyramid.

Don't wear your low pay as a badge of honour or pride.

Wear it as a badge of shame. Use it as a motivator to go forward, up the pyramid.

None of us can change the past.

We are where we are now, we've all made mistakes. However, recognise that if you're only pulling a grand or two out of your business each month, that's not right.

If you aspire to be a professional business owner, sat somewhere near the top of the pyramid, your business has to become capable of paying you professional business owner money.

To be clear, I recognise that money isn't the only thing.

I recognise that our businesses give us other things and have other purposes.

But while money isn't the only thing, it is an important thing.
You can't kid yourself that by taking out paltry levels of drawings on a monthly basis or going without pay every now and again so that everybody else gets paid except you somehow is a good thing, a necessary thing or a 'right of passage'.

It's not. It doesn't have to be like that. That's not a good thing.

In truth, it's a really clear beacon that you're an amateur business owner in the era of professional business owners.

The notion that there's a system here that could give you a pay rise every other month is a really smart thing.

I recognise that going from drawing £2,000 a month to drawing £10,000 a month is unlikely to happen in a couple of months, but it could be up to £3,000 a month in that time.

And this time next year, when you're gearing up to take £10,000 per month, the System will have worked.

Those prizes are what this System can do.

That's how you get the game-changing results.

You see, a new website on its own won't get you game-changing results.

A new CRM system on its own won't get you game-changing results.

However, the implementation of a system, executed properly by a business owner who's not stuck in the weeds, can and will get you those results.

When you implement it properly, it can change everything.

But it will take time. This is a minimum 12-month project.

Keeping an open mind is really important.

If your mind is closed to any of this, you're screwed.

That being said, just having an open mind isn't enough.

You've got to be able to implement.

It's the execution that will make the System work - not your knowledge of it.

Your understanding of the System is important, but your understanding will not deliver the results. It's your implementation and execution that delivers the results.

In that regard, as far as rhythmic acquisition of customers is concerned, it's always preceded by rhythmic activity.

The right activity happens rhythmically.

The rhythm in your business is really important.

In some businesses, there needs to be a fairly rapid rhythm. In other businesses, the rhythm can be a lot more measured, but it's still a rhythm.

We'll work out what your rhythm is.

But remember, you never ever get rhythmic acquisition of customers without rhythmic marketing activity.

You're going to have to put the activity in place.

If the rhythmic activity stops, we promise you that at some point the rhythmic acquisition will stop as well. Because one precedes the other. Always.

Woody Allen once said: *"If you want to make God laugh, tell him about your plans."*

At one level, this is true, but I prefer Eisenhower's quote. He said: *"In preparing for battle, I've always found that plans are useless, but planning is indispensable."*

We've got to start to play things through, understand things properly, look at what might happen and where it might take us.

Things will not go as you plan. They never do.

Some things might work better than you thought they would. Other things will work worse than you thought they would.

You need to understand that.

This is all about aim and direction.

What you need to do is take your time and think deeply about this stuff, about where you're going, and about this planning process. Our learning and our thinking determine our decisions.

The decisions that we make as a result of our learning and our thinking are what will end up determining our results.

And, our results will determine our future.

Your ability to take time and think deeply about this stuff and then make the right decisions are really important here.

Your results and performance next year will be equal to your skills and ability minus the interference that you allow in.

Your Results
=
Skills - Interference

If we think like an investor would think about our business, we're all capable of mapping out the plan to get us where we want to go.

What will get in the way is the other stuff – the interference.

The weeds.

As a business owner, you get to decide who gets your bandwidth and your time. Don't make those decisions lightly because the interference you allow in will diminish your results... and your progress up the pyramid towards where you've said you want to be.

Hopefully you can already see how this System is all joined together.

Wheel of Life

This is a useful exercise to help you understand your gap more clearly.

Take a look at the Wheel of Life:

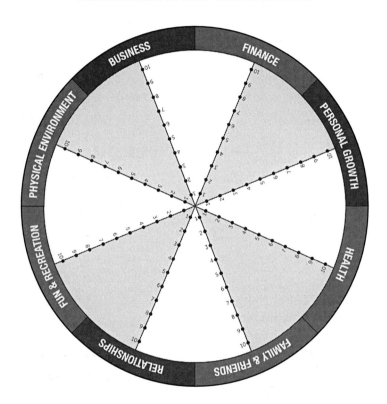

Look at each element of your life.

How happy are you with where your business is at right now?

How happy are you with where your finances are at right now?

How happy are you with your personal growth?

Your health?

Your relationships with family and friends?

Your personal relationship with your significant other?

How happy are you with your social life?

How happy are you with your physical environments? It could be where you live. It could be what you drive. It could be where you work. The physicality of where you spend your life – how happy are you with it?

On the wheel, mark each one of those things out of 10.

Don't spend too long thinking about it.

It should take you only about five or six minutes.

The purpose is to give us aim and direction and for us to understand what it is that's really important.

Some of you will have much greater deficiencies in elements like relationships or fitness, for instance, rather than your experience with business or finance.

This is a starting point to understanding where you are now and identifying the gap that we're going to close.

> ### *Download:*
> *Download your own wheel of life excercise sheets at:*
> ***EMSSystem.co.uk/downloads***

Final Thought for this Chapter:

There's a degree of comfort that comes from being in the weeds.

It's comfortable. Cosy.

But the price you'll pay when you're stuck in the weeds is that you won't execute the System or crack the rhythmic acquisition of customers.

The next twelve months won't be that much better than the previous twelve months for you.

The weeds keep you static on the pyramid. They inhibit any and all upward movement. 'Tis a heavy price to pay.

Get out of the weeds. Please.

CHAPTER THREE:
THE NUMBERS

"Numbers rule the universe"

Pythagoras

What goals did you set last year?

How did things work out for you?

What disappointments have you had this year?

You might be able to put on a front *(some can do that very successfully for very long periods of time)*, but you know whether your business is growing or shrinking. After all, there is no status quo.

It's okay that things didn't all go to plan. The trick is not to deny that.

Don't spin things.

Don't pretend that failures or bad things didn't happen.

Look at what's happened in your business in the past. Be honest about it and use that awareness and understanding to better shape the future.

Otherwise, you'll just go around again. You'll make the same mistakes.

And you'll have the same regrets.

So, if you've set big goals in the past but come up short, linger in that. Learn from that. Because therein lies the path to your future wealth and riches.

To be clear, sometimes things happen to you *(in business as well as in your personal lives)* that you can do nothing about. But what you can control is your response and reaction to them.

So when we look back, we're not trying to change the past. That's not the purpose at all!

You're just trying to learn from the mistakes that you made and things that you may have regretted, so you can shed proper light on what's going to happen in the future and how you'll behave and respond next time.

Four years ago, an Entrepreneurs Circle member had a major problem. He ignored a big VAT bill. He managed to ignore it for nearly 18 months until they turned up at his door. It caused a lot of pain and problems.

Luckily, he managed to get someone to invest some money to bail him out.

Over the next four years, he repaid that investment. The investor walked away and he was back in control of his business.

It was a happy story until he didn't pay his VAT bill again...

It's a recurring theme, because he's inept at managing the numbers in his business. When he's got cash in his bank account, he spends it.

When he had someone else who he had to be accountable to *(the investor)*, he was OK but the minute that person left, he regressed to his core state.

Everyone has recurring themes. Some of them aren't as drastic as this example, but everyone has them.

Your ability to be honest about them equips you to succeed going forward.

If you don't go back and pull out your previous plans and look at what actually came to pass you're denying yourself greater awareness and that will compromise your ability to plan effectively.

So don't skip this retrospective look back.

Those questions at the start of this chapter were not rhetorical.

It's not helpful for you if you're not making the most of what's happened historically.

It's part of your own proper self-awareness. Part of the planning, part of the process, part of your future success.

Once you know what your big weakness is, you can deal with it as a business owner. If you ignore it and kid yourself that somehow it isn't there, you'll just repeat it.

That's the purpose of looking back.

But, of course, we can also look forward.

How do you envisage the coming year going?
What are the things that you're excited about?
What are the things that you worry about?

The Numbers

What are the big things happening for your business?

As you start to shape your plan and close the gap, you have to do some proper planning. And to do that effectively you've got to understand your numbers.

Here's a little preamble about numbers:

The professional marketers follow you around the internet. They're advertising everywhere from Google to Facebook.

They're advertising while you're asleep at night. They're waiting for you in the morning.

They're the businesses you love to hate.

They're probably more successful than you.

You know why? Because their numbers don't care about your feelings.

You may have the greatest, most ethical business in the world. You might be able to literally heal the Earth, but without a well-designed marketing system, you're going to lose every time you come up against the big marketing gorillas who know their numbers.

But it doesn't have to be that way. When you properly know and understand your numbers you can play their game. You too can be a *'marketing gorilla'* in your market.

Let's look at two examples.

The first is a run-of-the-mill e-commerce campaign.

Let's say you get 1,000 unique visitors to your website.

You convert 1% into customers.

So 10 of them buy and the average spend is £50.

Your revenue is £500.

That's not very exciting unless your cost per click is less than 50p - which is unlikely.

Now compare that to this much smarter campaign:

You attract the same 1,000 visitors, but this time, rather than trying to sell straight away, you give away something on your web page. A really useful piece of content, say, and as a result your conversion rate goes up.

Now you get hundreds of leads and because you're educating people and helping them - you provide value. You increase their awareness of their problem which you can solve.

Your conversion rate jumps from 1% to 8 – 12%.
Now for the same advertising spend, you've got 30 sales totalling £1,500.

And this isn't even an optimised campaign.

You can add in additional marketing, upsells, downsells, post-sells, and continuity plans that can increase that £1,500 further.

If you have a big financial goal, but you don't know your numbers intimately, you're screwed.

This is why the professional marketers are winning in an era of professional business people.

They don't have better products than you.

Their services don't compare, BUT they understand the numbers.

Business, first and foremost, is about profit. Without profit, you can't market. And without marketing you'll never have the reach and the impact that you want.

For the Entrepreneurs Marketing System to work and for you to achieve what you want to achieve in business, you have to understand your numbers.

As my good friend Martin Norbury says:
"Business is a numbers game ... played by a team"

Your 12 Key Numbers

Yellow cells are input cells. only type in yellow cells!!
All yellow cells will calculate themselves once the yellows are inputted
The (small over) column will self calculate once you yellow cells are inputted

① Where are you NOW...

Top Down Model

		Now
1	Leads	2,000
	times	
2	Prospect Conversion	55%
	Equals	
3	Prospects	1,100
	times	
4	Customer Conversion	35%
	Equals	
5	No of Sales	385
	times	
6	Average Order value	£1,000
	Equals	
7	Total Revenue	£385,000
	times	
8	Gross Margin %	50%
	Equals	
9	Gross Profit	£192,500
	Less	
10	Overheads	£35,000
	Less	
11	Salaries	£30,000
	Equals	
12	Net Profit (before tax)	£127,500

② Small Hinges Swing Big Doors

Little Changes...

		% change	After
1	Leads	50%	3,000
2	Prospect Conversion	2%	57%
3	Prospects		1,710
4	Customer Conversion	3%	38%
5	No of Sales		650
6	Average Order value	5%	£1,050
7	Total Revenue		£682,290
8	Gross Margin %	3%	53%
9	Gross Profit		£361,614
10	Overheads	5%	£33,250
11	Salaries		£30,000
12	Net Profit (before tax)		£298,364

% Uplift in Net Profit	134%
Uplift in business value*	£1,030,000

③ Your Breakeven

Breakeven

1	675
2	55%
3	371
4	35%
5	130
6	£1,000
7	£130,000
8	50%
9	£65,000
10	£35,000
11	£30,000
12	£0

④ Profit First...

Bottom Up, Profit First Model

Tells you how many leads you need to achieve your target profit

		Now	After
1	No of Leads Needed	2,753	2184
	Equals		
2	Prospect Conversion	55%	57%
	Divided by		
3	Prospects	1,514	1245
	Equals		
4	Customer Conversion	35%	38%
	Divided by		
5	No of Sales	530	473
	Equals		
6	Average Order value	£1,000	£1,050
	Divided by		
7	Total Revenue	£530,000	£496,698
	Equals		
8	Gross Margin %	50%	53%
	Divided by		
9	Gross Profit	£265,000	£263,250
	Equals		
10	Overheads	£35,000	£33,250
	Plus		
11	Salaries	£30,000	£30,000
	Plus		
12	Target Net Profit (before tax)	£200,000	£200,000

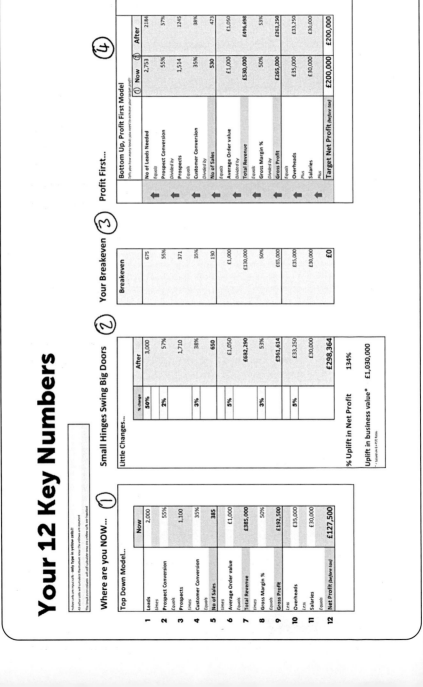

12 Key Numbers

There are 12 Key Numbers in every business and you can see them on this sheet *(opposite)*.

Your 12 Key Numbers are:

1. Leads

(This could be number of website visitors or number of homes that receive a flyer or number of visitors to your stand at a trade show etc. There are lots of variations depending on what business you are in and the type of marketing you're doing. In simple terms though, this is the number at the top of your funnel)

2. Prospect Conversion (%)

This is the rate at which you convert your leads into 'Prospects'.

(A Prospect is someone who, by their behaviour, has shown some interest in what it is that you do/sell. So, for instance, this could be people who have filled out your opt-in form on your website, or had a meeting with you, say)

3. Prospects

We've defined prospects, above.

You have to nurture your leads.

Your ability to nurture your leads via your funnel can become a critical factor in the success of your marketing and the rhythmic acquisition of customers.

*(You can download the spreadsheet opposite and all the other tools referenced in this book at **EMSSystem.co.uk/downloads**)*

You can, for example, send them videos, emails, or you might even phone them.

The goal is to convert more of those leads into prospects.

What makes someone a prospect as opposed to a lead will vary by business. In our business, for instance, a lead becomes a prospect when they have a Discovery Call/ Meeting with us. In other words, the lead is the very raw person who comes in at the top of your funnel. The prospect is when the next major thing happens, such as a phone call or a meeting, say.

4. Customer Conversion (%)

Not all your prospects will become customers. The rate at which you convert prospects to customers is your Customer Conversion; a critical number for you because it determines how many prospects *(and therefore how many leads)* you need in order to hit your goals.

5. Number of Sales

This is probably the most straightforward number on the list. It's the number of sales you make.

6. Average Order Value

If each time we've asked a business owner *"What's your average order value?"* and been given a £1 coin for every time someone has replied *"It varies..."* we'd be millionaires many times over. The truth is... it doesn't vary! There's always an average. We get that the actual transaction size varies. Some customers spend a lot and others spend a little, sure. But the Average Order Value is simply the total value of your sales, divided by the number of transactions. Simple.

Every business has variances in transaction size. But every business also has an Average Order Value and it's your job to know what yours is.

7. Total Revenue

Again, this one's nice and easy. For the purposes of our spreadsheet, this one's simply a sum of the **Number of Sales** multiplied by the **Average Transaction Value.**

Advice about 'rounding'.

The absolute, exact, to the penny, number doesn't really matter when it comes to your twelve Key Numbers. In our business, we work everything to the nearest £1,000. You might work to the nearest £100.
And we NEVER go to decimal places.
On anything on this sheet.
The secret to this is the big picture.

8. Gross Margin Percentage

This is the share of each sale that you get to 'keep' in your business to contribute towards your overheads and your profit.

For example, if I'm selling tables and I buy my tables for £60 and sell them for £100, then my Gross Margin Percentage is 40% because 40% *(£40)* of every sale *(£100)* is mine to keep after I've paid for the goods *(£60)*.

Now, it can be really helpful to get quite sophisticated with this number, and add into the 'costs' all sums that are only 'spent' when you make sales. In the best case, this would include your marketing costs once you have your System in place and your marketing returns are predictable.

It would also definitely include all sub-contracted costs that you only incur when you make a sale. So for instance, if you had a sub-contracted joiner who assembled the tables and you only paid him when you had a table to build and he charged £10 per table, then you'd include those costs in your Gross Margin Percentage. So in the example above, your Gross Margin Percentage would come down to 30% because your costs are now £60 for the table and £10 to build it *(so £70 in total)* from your £100 sale.

(Be careful here. If your joiner is on payroll and you had to pay him regardless of how many tables you sold, then his/her costs would be included in the salaries line below).

The beautiful thing about your Gross Margin Percentage is that once you've passed break-even point, this is the amount that your profit grows by every time you make a sale. It's that knowledge that can be liberating for your marketing when you understand it properly.

9. Gross Profit

This is the amount of money you have left to fund your overheads, salaries and profit AFTER all your 'direct costs' have been paid.

On our spreadsheet, this is a sum of the Total Revenue line times by the Gross Margin Percentage.

The minute you get beyond break-even, your gross profit goes straight to the bottom line because all your fixed costs are covered.

This means that once you get beyond break-even with a business, you can do a lot more. You can spend more to get customers and grow. Once you're beyond break-even, you can be a lot more bullish with your marketing push to acquire market share and more customers.

10. Overheads

These are your fixed costs. In other words, all the costs you have to pay regardless of whether you sell one table or 1,000 tables. This is where you'll include all your rent, vehicle costs, utilities etc. Don't include your payroll costs here. We highlight them separately below.

11. Salaries

These are your people costs. To begin with, you would include in here all your costs of everyone you pay UNLESS they only get paid when you make a sale *(in which case they'd be included in your Gross Margin Percentage above)*.

If they expect to be paid at the end of the week or month regardless of how many sales you've made, then their costs go in here.

12. Net Profit *(before tax)*

This is what's actually left for you, after you've paid all your costs.

Now, what's important about all the numbers is that they are all linked.

For example, net profit + salaries + overheads = gross profit.

Your gross profit is a margin of your total revenue.

Your total revenue comes from the number of sales you make and the Average Order Value.

Your sales will come from prospects which in turn come from leads. Everything is linked.

> ## ****IMPORTANT****
> On the downloadable spreadsheet you should only input numbers into the yellow boxes. All the other cells will automatically compute based on what you put in those yellow boxes.

The Aeroplane Analogy

The key thing to understand is that all these numbers are directly linked together. So when you change one of them, all the others change too.

The System depends upon those elements all being joined together and on you, the business owner, knowing and understanding what each of your 12 Key Numbers are.

Donald Miller has a really good analogy about business. He likened a business to an aeroplane.

The wings of the plane are your products and services because without products and services, you've got nothing to sell. You've got no lift. It's the wings that give the business lift and get you in the air.

Your marketing efforts and marketing spend are the thrust that drives you forward, giving you the lift and getting the whole plane in the air.

But your overheads are your fuselage. They're just trying to bring your aeroplane back down to the ground.

If you have little tiny wings and a massive fuselage, the business never gets flying.

Similarly, you can have really big wings but if the fuselage gets bigger, it all starts coming down because you can't create enough thrust to keep it in the air.

If you have big wings, lots of thrust and an appropriate size fuselage though, you've got a very effective plane that can fly you anywhere.

The way to build significant growth in most businesses is to get a little bit better, right through the chain of 12 Key Numbers. So you improve all, or most, of them by a little bit.

When you do that, the compound impact can be exponential.

Now it's possible sometimes to get a lot better in one or two places, but more frequently the smart way is just to tweak three or four elements by a small percentage.

So you've got a picture as to what needs to happen in your business to generate the profitability that you want.

It might make you realise 'Gosh I'm not that far away from where I want to be... I could get there'.

For others it might be 'I can never get there. The gap is too big. My business as it's currently structured isn't congruent with one that can deliver the profitability that I need'.

Even that's a good thing to realise because it means you're going to stop putting effort into something that will never work. This level of clarity is key for the System to work.

If you start to move forward with big ambition and big plans and you're serious about joining this era of the professional business person, you have to get to grips with these numbers.

It's not that complicated.

When you were learning to drive, you sat down behind the wheel of a car for the first time and you were incompetent. You didn't know what to do.

But you got there.

It didn't really take that long. You just had to put in a few hours with someone who knew what they were doing and all of a sudden you could drive a car.

It's no different with these numbers.

Once you understand it, you can apply it to any business. It's a life skill that you'll have forever.

It's also an entry requirement to the era of the professional business person.

You have to know this stuff.

Download the 12 Key Numbers & watch our Video tutorials at:
EMSSystem.co.uk/numbers

CHAPTER FOUR:
THE GAP

"The gap between where you are now and where you want to be is where the magic happens – in business and in life"

As business owners in this era of the professional business person, you have to know your numbers.

"Business is a numbers game played by a team."

If you aren't playing a numbers game, you aren't playing a professional business game.

You're an enthusiastic amateur.

There's nothing wrong with that per se. It's just that the rewards at an amateur level aren't as great as they are at professional level.

Amateur business people are in the bottom half of the pyramid.

Professional business people are in the top half of the pyramid.

One of the big differences between amateurs and professionals in business is their grasp of the right numbers.

The pro's have it. The amateurs don't.

We often say that:

marketing
=
creativity + maths

Which means you can't ignore the maths.

If you run your business superficially, without care or depth of thought to your numbers, then you'll never sustainably be in the top echelons of the pyramid. It's simply not possible.

Without the grasp of the right numbers you'll make poor quality decisions.

The decisions that you take will shape your future.

So, this does matter.

For instance, there are three magic numbers that you must know going forward for this system to work:

1. What does it cost you to acquire a customer now?
2. What it could cost you to acquire a customer if/when you know your numbers?
3. How much is that customer worth?

If you don't know those numbers or you guess and make them up, the System won't work. You'll make bad decisions and you'll stay down the bottom half of the pyramid.

You have to work out what it costs you *(currently)* to acquire a customer and how much that customer is worth.

You don't have to know to the absolute pence or even pound, but you should know within ten pounds what it costs to acquire a customer.

When it comes to how happy entrepreneurs are with their business and financial wealth, most business owners aren't scoring 10 out of 10 on the Wheel of Life.

The way to correct that is to ask yourself

"Well, what could my life be like?".

Let us explain...

On the day you started out, you had a goal.

You had a dream.

You had something that you wanted to achieve.

Unfortunately, for most people, somewhere between that first day in business and the present day, they've lost sight of that goal. They've compromised on it.

They've got stuck in the weeds.

They set off going to London and actually they're now somewhere off the Isles of Scilly.

But you're a business owner. There's no one telling you what to do. You haven't got a boss.

All you have to do is reconnect with your goals. You can recalibrate, start again and get yourself to where you want to be.

The reason most people never reach their goals is because they don't define them.

They don't write them down. They don't sit down and do some proper thinking about where they actually want to be.

This is important because your thinking determines your decisions.

Your decisions determine your results.
Your results determine your lifestyle and where you end up.

Just like our twelve numbers, these things are all linked together and they're what makes the difference when it comes to your place on the pyramid.

So you'd better start thinking about what you actually want to achieve. Truthfully.

Being able to meet payroll this month or pay the VAT bill when it falls due isn't really a goal that's worthy of a professional business person.

What we found most helpful is not to start with where you are now.

Instead, start with where you want to be.

My life changed in 2002. I had a successful corporate career and was employed at the time as the managing director of someone else's business.

My wife, Sue, had booked an appointment for us to go and look around Solihull School. Now, neither Sue or I went to a fee-paying school. Never until that point did we have any notion that our children might go to a fee-paying school.

We met the headmaster and were given a tour of the school and my mind was completely blown.

My only point of reference was the comprehensive school in Leeds that I'd attended. All of a sudden I saw this incredible place with all these facilities and this amazing environment.

That afternoon changed my life. I now wanted to send my kids to that school. But there was a problem...

The school fees required a lot of money! We had four children. The fees for four children were £50,000 a year, after tax.

Although I had a well-paid job *(I was earning a six-figure salary working for somebody else)*, there was no way I could contemplate putting my children into Solihull School in my current situation.

So he had to rethink what he was doing.

I did the numbers and worked out what earnings I needed. It was a sizeable six-figure sum.

Realistically, I wasn't going to earn that working for somebody else. At least, not in the time frame needed.

The clock was ticking – I couldn't extend the deadline!

This triggered me to hand in my notice, leave corporate life and set up my own business.

I was blissfully naive at the time.

My last salary was £130,000 a year. My logic was really simple: *"If I could earn £130,000 a year working for somebody else, I must be able to earn more than that working for myself."*

"Looking back, I'm very grateful that I was blissfully ignorant, because it meant I entered entrepreneurship with quite different expectations to most people. I had a clear goal and I was totally focused on it."

Sue & I took a punt and remortgaged our house before I handed in my resignation.

We took £100,000 out on the mortgage so we had some money to live on while we built the business.

"At the time, it didn't terrify me at all, because I knew a lot less than I know now. But that was a really good thing.

I had a very simple goal. The deal I had with Sue was that we needed £100,000 cash in the first year to move from our company account into our personal account. If I did this in the first year, I could carry on running my own business."

"If I didn't do it in the first year, I'd have to go back and get another job while I was still employable."

"My drive was that I wanted to put the kids into Solihull School. It's quite a big decision to put your kids into a private school but I promise you, it's an even bigger decision to take them out. Once you've put them in, you're going to do anything you can to keep them there. Of course, when you own a business, that means making your business more successful."

"You have to find and plug into something that matters to you. The more it matters, the more successful you'll be."

Sometimes that means we have to get creative as business owners. We have to create stuff that matters.

We've found, historically, that the more holidays we book, the more successful our business is.

Those things aren't unconnected. The more lavish our holidays are, the more successful our business is. It has to be because it has to pay for the holidays.

If you have young children then all kids want to go to Disney. It's an amazing thing to do but it costs at least £10,000 for a family of four to go to Walt Disney World in Florida and do it properly.

Most people aren't used to spending £10,000 on a holiday. But as a business owner, you can do that.

The trick is to book the holiday a year ahead of when you're going to go. Then tell everybody that you know that you're going on the holiday because then you've got some skin in the game. You can't cancel that holiday! And you've got nine or ten months to generate the cash to pay the balance when it falls due.

Now your business will grow because you'll do the right things because you HAVE to pay for the holiday. You can't cancel the holiday because you've already told the kids.

Over 200 *'EC families'* have gone to Disney using the above technique. We heartily recommend it. And if Disney's not your thing, book the Maldives, the Great Wall of China, or the luxurious cruise that you've always coveted. Do what works for you but recognise the power of this lever.

Being a business owner means that you have the ability to define what your life is like.

It isn't up to anybody else. You can do it.

You can choose where you want to live, what you want to drive, what you want to spend your money on, where you go on holiday, where you eat out etc.

Every single thing about your lifestyle as a business owner is down to you.

But for that to happen, you have to recognise and take ownership of it.

You have to map out and be prepared to write down your goals and what you want.

Meet Glenn and David...

When Glenn and David first came to Entrepreneurs Circle with their fledgling hybrid estate agency EweMove, they'd only just started the business. But on the first day, they already knew what the end point was.

They said, *"We started this business six months ago. We're going to sell it for £12 million six years from now. Everything we're going to do between now and then is to make that happen."*

They were incredibly focused.

But they failed...

Instead, they sold it for £15million after only five years.

So, they got there a year earlier and took £3 million more than they set out to do.

Their secret: they started with the end in mind.

If I could bestow one thing on every single person reading this book, it would be for you to be able to articulate the end that you have in mind.

Where are you going?
What are you building?
What's the goal?

Part of the problem, for many, is you don't know where you want to be.

When you don't know where you want to be, it doesn't matter what you do.

But you can build the life you want for the people who matter to you and for yourself IF you define it.

You have to design it, cost it, transpose it into your business and then create the business plan.

Boom. Do that and your ascension up the pyramid will be all but assured.

Think about it. You have two choices: you can make a living or you can design a life.

It's great when you design a life. It's a really cool thing to do. We heartily recommend it.

And it can be really helpful to start outside of work.

One of the smartest things that I've ever done was to get a housekeeper. I never thought of getting a housekeeper, but getting a housekeeper has been one of the very best things in my life. She does everything: food shopping, laundry, cleaning, changing light bulbs, etc.

She comes in for 25 hours every week.

It changes your life!

Life's better when you don't have to do the menial stuff.

When I come home in the evening, Sue's not doing ironing and so we can be together. They can be with the kids, because all the chores have been taken care of. When you design your ideal life, I would recommend some form of domestic assistance!

Think about where you want to live, where you want to travel and where you want to go on holiday.

Include all the things like private healthcare, cars, school fees, housekeepers, gardeners, gym memberships, personal trainers, etc.

Let yourself go. Start to paint the picture that YOU want.

And then you start to cost it.

You have to know what it's going to cost.

A wish list is nice, but wishes tend not to come true.

Things only come true when they really matter.

How do you turn it from a wish list into something that's much more real?

The short answer is that you have to commit to it.

The best way we know of committing is to go public with it by starting to tell people who matter to you. The more public you go with it, the more likely that it will happen.

If you're playing to win, you go public.

Tell everybody about the holiday that you've booked as you've now got to do things in the business in order to pay for it. There's something that you now must achieve.

It's much easier not to 'go public' of course. But the price you pay for NOT doing it is you slash your chances of making it happen. Whatever it might be.

What we've seen is that those who play not to lose, broadly speaking, don't lose anything other than the life that they could've lived.

But in many ways this is the biggest loss of all isn't it.

A life unlived. Dreams unfulfilled. A lifestyle diminished.

This is big stuff.

There's all this potential and opportunity, but the only reason you haven't had it yet is because you chose to play it safe. You didn't work it out, or write it down, or commit by telling others about your goals.

To be clear, I'm not advocating cavalier risk-taking here.

You have to be sensible and measured about this.

You can do it in little blocks.
You can start to talk about the plans and where they go.

The smart thing is don't move to a much bigger house, hire a housekeeper, book the holiday and order three flashy cars all at the same time. That would be foolish.

Just do one of them to start with!

Prioritise and then move forward. Purposefully.
But failing even to attempt to define your ideal life means that you're playing not to lose.

Now I'm not judging you. But I wouldn't be doing my job if I didn't point out to you the price you're paying when you play not to lose.

People who play not to lose never win.

Football teams that play not to lose don't win trophies. They may preserve their Premier League status. They may remain mediocre *(which is success of a sort)*, but they don't win.

Your ability to sit and reflect with a pen in hand and write it down is the first indicator to know if you're ever going to close your gap.

If you don't write down your goals then there is no gap.

If there's no gap, you're playing not to lose.

That means you can't ever win.

Once you've worked out and written down where you want to be, the next step is to take that cost of your ideal life and transpose it onto your business.

You put in your target net profit *(the money you need to fund the lifestyle you've created)* and now, you've defined your gap.

You now know what you've got to do.

For example, for you to pull a net profit of £200,000, you might need 3,300 leads. That works out to 60 leads a week or nine leads a day. Thus, if you can get nine leads a day, you can live your dream life.

Now you've got a purpose.

This is how successful entrepreneurs think and plan.

This is how professional business owners at the top of the pyramid think and behave.

It's NOT how amateur business people think and plan.

Amateur business people don't plan.

They tell themselves that they can't do these numbers.

They don't understand that the 12 Key Numbers are all linked together in a closed loop.

They've never written down the life that they wanted to live.

Instead they blunder on, doing the best they can, coping with today's emergency and this week's crisis. They live a life embedded and entwined in the weeds.
Their focus is on the weeds. Not the leads.

Good planning is always simple.

Design your ideal life without worrying about the costs at this point.

Just map out what you'd like your life to look like.

Then, when you've mapped it all out, start to put a cost against it.

You then transpose that cost onto the business: i.e the business needs to produce this much net profit to fund the lifestyle that I've defined.

Then we use the 12 Key Numbers sheet to work backwards from the desired net profit figure to calculate the sales, the leads, the margins etc that are needed to deliver your goal.

Now sometimes the goals need to be checked to ensure they make sense.

There are four elements to checking your goals/gap:

1. Operational Capacity

Let's just think for a minute...

If you're an accountant and you're the only fee-earning guy in your practice, you haven't got the capacity to look after 500 clients by yourself. So, if your goal requires 500 clients, something's got to give.

You have two options at this point:

You can start to move your price point up so your number of clients required comes down to a level you could manage on your own.

Or...

You could increase your costs and employ other people to do the work, but then your margins change.

2. Marketing

Where are these customers going to come from?

Where am I going to get the number of leads I need per week from? Is that feasible?

Sometimes you won't know the answer to that yourself. You may have to seek input or help from an expert.

3. Selling Capacity

Have you got the capacity to make the sales needed.

This will be a blocker for some people, because you're the person who does the work AND the selling. So, if the number of new sales you need is really high, you've hit a problem again.

You can't have that many sales meetings as you've all this work to do, so you have to look at solutions that have been discussed above.

4. You need to check if achieving your goal is even possible.

Usually, there'll be people who are better equipped than you to do the sense-check.

The person who's better equipped will rarely be your accountant *(there are exceptions - but it's rare!)*

Accountants, by nature, are typically very cautious. They'll see the worst. They typically play not to lose.

You need that sometimes, but when it comes to sense-checking goals, it can be really fruitless.

You want someone who's able to see the possibilities as well as the constraints to understand whether or not your goals are doable.

It's much better to have fewer goals than lots of goals. It's not about having 20 different marketing pillars running on 20 different media channels at the same time.

It's about focusing on a maximum of three marketing pillars at any one time.

If you get those three working better then you can go onto another one, and another, and another.

But if you start to impact four or five or six marketing pillars all at once, it will be too demanding and challenging. Corners will get cut. Details will get missed and things will start to fall apart.

CHAPTER FIVE:
THE CALCULATOR

"A good businessman is a hybrid of a dancer and a calculator"

Paul Valery

How much **_should_** you be spending to get a customer?

What's your current marketing cost per lead?
(By the way, it will be different by marketing pillar!)

Amateur business people don't know the answers to those questions.

But in the era of the professional business person – especially if you're wanting to move up the pyramid and crack the rhythmic acquisition of customers - the answers to those questions become really important.

Have a look at this email that I received from an Entrepreneurs Circle member recently:

"Could really have some help on our Facebook campaign...

We've been running an offer for a one-month free trial for the last seven weeks.

Quickly became apparent that leads are generated over weekends so we only run the campaign from Friday to Monday.

Budget is currently set at £15 a day for those three days.

We tried £7.50, then £10, and finally began to get leads at around £15.

It's generating on average one lead per weekend. We've had seven leads so far.

Cost per lead is currently £42.37.

Please, can you help us work out what to do?"

As a professional business person, what would your advice be to this budding entrepreneur?

The answer, of course, is that you need to know some other information.

So, what other information might you want to know?

Well, the value of a customer would be really helpful.

Ok, I can tell you that each customer spends an average of £300 per month – and they pay by direct debit. Gross Margin is around 50%.

And how many of those leads became customers is a critical piece that we're missing.

Good point – you're right. I can tell you that three of the seven leads have become customers.

So things are a lot clearer now...

...well, yes, they are but it'd be really good to know how many months, on average, a new customer stays with the business?

The answer is 20 months.

Cool. Now we have everything.

So the business has spent £296 *(7 leads at £42.37 each)*.

For that they've acquired THREE new customers, who will each pay £300 each for, on average, the next 20 months. So that's £900 of revenue, for 20 months = £18,000 of revenue...

...at a gross margin of 50% = £9,000 contribution.

For a spend of £296.

Even an enthusiastic amateur business person can see that when you do the maths, it's obvious what to do. Run more ads. Spend more money.

This person is pretty much an alchemist because they're investing £296 and turning it into £900 in the first month. That's a 300% return on investment – in one month.

Warren Buffett is basically the most genius investor ever and he's happy with 25% return on investment in a whole year. Yet this marketing campaign is generating 300% in a MONTH and the person running it couldn't see it. Because he didn't do the maths.

Couldn't happen in your business could it?

When you understand the numbers, the answer is crystal clear.

In fact, crystal is opaque in comparison!

Part of the Entrepreneurs Marketing System is the Marketing Spend Calculator.

It's fairly straightforward, but it requires a bit of thought.

Your Marketing Spend Calculator

1. How much is your average customer worth to you?
Over their lifetime or the next 2-3 years, say.
£ _____

2. How much would you pay to get one of those customer?
Taking into account their lifetime value above.
£ _____

3. How many leads do you need to get a customer?
*If you sell to half the people you speak to, you would need
2 leads to get 1 customer. What's your ratio?*
_____

4. How much can you spend to get a lead?
Answer 2 divided by Answer 3.
£ _____

5. How many new customers do you want next month?
_____

**6. How many leads do you need next month to get
that many customers?**
Answer 3 x Answer 5.
_____

**7. How much marketing spend do you need for the next
month to get that many customers?**
Answer 6 x Answer 4.
£ _____

The first thing you need to know when you're working out your Marketing Spend Calculator is how much your average customer is worth to you over the time that they're going to spend with you.

This will vary, obviously, but for every business there's an average which you'll need to work out.

Download:
*you can download this exercise and all the other tools referenced
in this book at: **https://EMSSystem.co.uk/downloads***

Then, you want to know how much you would pay to get one of those customers.

The keywords are *"you would pay"*, taking into account their lifetime value.

This is where it gets a little bit subjective. It's where, as entrepreneurs, we sometimes can't think sufficiently deeply and can come up with wrong answers.

How much you would pay to get a customer can be impacted by factors like access to cash. In theory, you'd be prepared to spend £X but you haven't got enough £X to actually do it. Your business is under-capitalised.

Next, you work out how many leads you need to get a customer.

You have to understand what proportion of your leads, that come in at the top, flow through to your sales line.

Now, you need to know the ratios for your business. How many leads need to come in? This is where a lot of amateur business people start to comment and form judgement on what they call the quality of their leads. Because they're not getting the chequebook or the credit card out straight away and spending money, these business owners are dismissing them as poor-quality leads.

These people are amateurs when it comes to marketing and growing a business. What they're looking for is people to see a Facebook ad and spend money straight away. That does happen, but only in a fairly small percentage of cases.

The Calculator

To convert more of your leads you'll need to nurture them, putting good stuff out there of value, and pull people closer. That's how you build a big business.

The professional business person understands that and is prepared to embrace it.

Not everybody that comes in will buy in week one or month one, or even month two. But you're going to stay in touch, nurture those people and more of them will buy from you eventually.

Number four on the Marketing Spend Calculator is how much can you spend to get a lead.

The good news is that you don't have to guess, because you now can work it out.

You take the answer for how much you would pay to get a customer and you divide it by your answer for how many leads you need to get a customer.

Ta da!

It's straightforward. There's no guessing required. It's just a sum.

Number five on the Marketing Spend Calculator is how many customers do you want next month. Easy – that'll be defined by your gap and how big your growth targets are.

Number six on the Marketing Spend Calculator is another sum because you just multiply how many leads you need to get a customers *(Box 3)* by the number of customers you want next month *(Box 5)*.

Finally, the last box is how much do you need to spend on your marketing for the next month to get that many customers – which is your answer in Box 6 multiplied by your answer in Box 4.

You've just applied a bit of science, but you've now started to get some proper intelligence as to what you could and should be spending to get customers.

This starts to shape a lot of things!

If you don't understand these numbers or you forget the maths part of marketing *(remember, marketing is creativity plus the maths)*, you're an amateur business person as opposed to a professional business person.

You're not going to be able to take control of your destiny and move your business to where you want to get it without using this Calclulator properly. You have to get a grasp on those numbers!

The most useful way to do it – always – is to start with the end in mind.

For example, lets say you're at £45,000 per month in revenue and want to be at £100,000 per month.

We'd break down the deficit of £55,000 and figure out exactly how to get there...by working backwards.

Now, let's just say your average client is worth, I don't know... hmmm £3,000 per month.

Then you'd need an extra 19 clients *(rounded up from £18,333)* to hit that number.

And we'll say that you're not in any crazy rush or anything... and want to get there, in like the next 6 months.

That'd be three new clients per month, but we'll chuck an extra one in there for good measure and some churn.

Meaning you need one new client per week.

Now... we'd look at how many new leads you'd need in order to land one new client per week.

If you're like most businesses you'd need around four leads per week. Five tops!

Easy peasy pudding and pie.

Then, we'd work out how much traffic you'd need to get to your landing pages on your website to generate five highly-qualified leads.

And how much we'd be able to afford to *'buy'* that traffic...

And still make sure there is enough money left over at the end of the month to pay all your bills - including your increased drawings.

Look, we've got this down to a science. A System.

It's not guesswork.

At the top of the pyramid, marketing is not *"crossing our fingers and hoping for the best"*.

Dan Sullivan said, *"The skills that got you out of Egypt aren't the ones that get you to the promised land."*

So, all the experience and the knowledge that have enabled you to get your business to where it is today aren't the same skills that will turn that business into one that's generating significantly more profit for you.

You're going to need a different set of skills.

You're going to need a different way of thinking.

The people who are using the same skills today as they were one, two or five years ago, are the ones who are stuck in the weeds and, as you already know, you've got to get out of the weeds.

Why are you running your business?

What's it all about?

What are you building here?

Design that life.

The Calculator

Understand why it matters.

Cost it.

Transpose it onto your business.

Then, the clear goal starts to emerge.

CHAPTER SIX:
THE FOUNDATIONS

"Without solid foundations you'll have great trouble creating anything of value..."

All of us have travelled somewhere.

We've stayed away from home for some periods of time.

Let's think about these five scenarios:

1. Ian is going on a six-week trip to Australia.
2. Neil has this beautiful place in the Alps and he's going skiing for a week.
3. Scott likes to relax on the beach so he's going for a fortnight to Barbados.
4. Jackie is going to see her mum for a night.
5. Brian is away on business for two nights.

Five different people. Five different trips.

But there are certain things that they're all going to take with them.

Scott isn't going to take his woolly hat to the Caribbean and Jackie doesn't need to pack a lot as she's only going away for one night.

But there are certain things that they all need, regardless of the trip they're going on.

They're all going to pack some pants, socks, toiletries, and a charger.

There are certain basics that we all need, no matter how short or long our trip is. Whether it costs ten grand or ten pounds, we're all going to take the same 'basics' with us.

Pants, socks, toiletries and a charger. Everyone. Always. Whatever the trip.

They're our 'foundations'.

And when it comes to marketing a business – any business – we have the equivalent of these foundations; a few elements that every professional business person will have in place. That's why we call them the Foundation Blocks.

It doesn't matter what your goal is or where on the pyramid you want to end up, there are certain foundations that you need in place in order to properly crack the rhythmic acquisition of customers and systemise your marketing.

They're the marketing equivalent of your pants, socks, toiletries and chargers. They're your Foundation Blocks.

The Foundation Blocks in the Entrepreneur's Marketing and Sales System help build the infrastructure for proper professional marketing in any business.

No one gets a pass on the Foundation Blocks.

There are 11 Blocks that I've defined in this System and we'll look at each of them in turn:

1. Marketing Asset Review
2. Google My Business
3. Follow-up Process
4. Remarketing and Pixel Tracking

5. Price Review
6. Systemised Collection of Reviews
7. Marketing Calendar
8. Knowledge Centre
9. Neighbourhood Cards
10. LinkedIn
11. Answering Your Phone
    (obvious, we know, but you'll be surprised!)

It's possible that your business won't need all 11, but you'll need to go through them to understand them before you're able to make that decision. Skip forward at your peril!

To be clear, if you decide to jettison a Foundation Block because it doesn't apply to you, please make sure you do it consciously from a well-informed perspective.

1. Your Marketing Asset Review

Let's be honest with each other: most marketing, put out by most businesses, isn't very good. And quite a lot of it is rubbish.

There ought to be some standard by which your marketing assets and collateral can be objectively assessed.

Well, now there is. We've created it.

Now, at one level, the only standard that really matters is the results that the particular piece of marketing generates. But very few businesses have any kind of robust tracking in place and so they're left with uninformed, subjective assessments as to whether their marketing is OK or not.

Marketing Collateral Quality Test

Run this test against all your individual marketing pieces.
Website, flyers, ads – the principles apply to them all. Are you 'up to scratch'?
Score each item out of 10 and then total for a score out of 100.

1. Crystal Clear Objective
What's the purpose of this marketing piece?
What does it want people to do? Is it obvious?

2. Not Boring
Is it the same as everyone else in your market?
If you replaced your logos with your competitors would it still make sense?
Is the language 'normal', not corporate, or uppity?
Are the Images interesting and creative and not 'same-old, same-old' cliched stock pics?
Will they remember anything about it 10 minutes after they've stopped reading/visiting?

3. Clear Positioning
Is it obvious and clear why they should choose you over your competitors?
Does it contain helpful stuff that's useful and shows you are an 'authority'?

4. Personable & Relatable
People buy people, remember...
Are you in/on it?
Does it include photos & videos of you and your team?

5. Video
No excuses. No inhibitions. It's time. You need both of these:
- You and your team, being helpful and 'passionately educating' your prospects?
- Your clients talking about you on video?Does it include photos & videos of you and your team?

6. Awards/Accreditations
If you've got it, flaunt it. Do not hide any lights under any bushels!

7. Links to independent Review sites
Showcase the reviews and stars you have on whichever site/s is most relevant for your sector.
E.g. Google, TripAdvisor, Trustpilot, thebestof, etc.
Absolutely essential for almost every business. Mustn't be missed out.

8. Testimonials
Not as good as reviews from independent sites but useful nonetheless.
Must be PROPERLY displayed to count. That means:
photo, name and a headline that summarises message.
Rule for website: At least 4 testimonials for every year you've been in business

9. Strong Offer
Is there a strong reason for them to take action now?

10. Multiple, clear, 'Calls To Action'
"At least four, probably more..."

Total Score

Let's say you run a leaflet campaign and you drop 10,000 leaflets and you only get three phone calls as a result. Is the leaflet at fault or is it leaflet campaigns *(the media)* that won't/doesn't work for you?

Same with your website or an advert in a magazine. How do you know whether it's the media that's not working or the particular piece of collateral.

One way to work that out is to go through the EC Marketing Collateral Quality Test.

This is a quality test for people who aspire to be a professional business person.

The Test assesses the quality of each of your marketing pieces and you can complete it yourself in around five minutes for each one.

You should run this test against all your individual marketing pieces like your website, flyers, and ads.

Lets look at each element in the Test:

Crystal Clear Objective

Most of the collateral that we see fails at the first principle. They've lost track and sight of their objective.

Let's say you're going to send some direct mail. The objective of the letter or piece is to get a meeting. So, on that basis then, you don't need to sell your product or service in that letter. The purpose of the letter isn't to sell your product or service. It's to sell the meeting and the reasons why the prospect should meet with you, which is very different to trying to sell the product.

Same with a lot of websites. The objective of many is to get the prospect to ring you – yet the website is all about selling the product not the call.

It should be so blindingly obvious what any particular piece of marketing is trying to get the reader/viewer to do.

Is it driving traffic to a website?

Do you want people to give you a call?

Do you want them to download a particular piece of collateral?

Only in some cases will it actually be to buy the product/service.

What's the purpose?

What does it want people to do?

All marketing is about persuading people – your prospects – to take action.

The clearer the objective is within the copy, the more clarity you have around what you want people to do, and the more people will do it.

Not Boring

The second principle of the Test is that the piece shouldn't be boring.

So much marketing that's churned out, especially from small or medium-sized businesses, is devoid of any original or creative thought. It's same-old same old, dull as ditchwater.

Is it the same as everyone else in your market?

Are you doing what everyone else is doing?

Will the reader/viewer of your marketing piece remember anything about it 10 minutes after they've put it down or will it blend into the sea of sameness and unremarkability?

The professional business person wouldn't let their marketing do that. They'd be different in some way – and you must be too.

One way to assess whether you're doing the same as everyone else in your market is to replace your logo with your competition's logo. Would everything still make sense? You'd be surprised how often that's the case!

If the answer is yes, you're failing this part of the Quality Test.

There needs to be something that's different and unique to you.

One way to do that is with the words you use.

So many businesses get the language wrong in their marketing.

They use corporate speak or talk professionally.

Whereas in most markets now, the more human and real you're

able to be, the more people will relate to what you're saying and the better your response will be.

And then there are the images.

We have a very straightforward rule for our monthly magazine, the EC Circular; if an image could appear in the local Chamber of Commerce magazine, it's not going in mine.

That's our criteria. We don't want any boring images in our Circular.

So many people, and especially if you use any kind of design business or web design company, use boring images by default.

That's because their default customers aren't as savvy as you are.

From a marketing perspective, most businesses are amateurs when it comes to marketing so they copy what everyone else does and as a result their marketing looks like everyone elses. They don't stand out, are not seen as different, and find it perpetually hard to get customers. They're stuck in the lower half of the pyramid.

But you recognise that the images in your marketing collateral are an important attention-grabber.

Once you know that you can't use the same old type of images as everyone else, you want something that's interesting and attention grabbing.

Will they remember anything about your marketing piece 10 minutes after they've put it down?

If you actually create something that's impactful and engaging, it will resonate with people and they will remember it – for a little while at least.

You're rarely the best person to run the 'Not-Boring-Test' on your own marketing.

At least in the beginning, you need a helping hand from someone honest and objective.

If you get your marketing collateral right, everything else is really easy.

But if your marketing collateral is mediocre, everything else becomes a lot harder.

This is a key point of leverage for the entire System.

Clear Positioning

Is it obvious why your customer or potential customer should choose you over your competitors?

Seriously. Why should they spend their hard earned cash with you, as opposed to all the other choices they have?
So many small businesses provide excellent service. They really care about each customer. But their marketing doesn't reflect that and they throw away what is a major competitive advantage.

How is your marketing piece positioning you?

You somehow need to show that you're top of the tree.

You need something that says you're the best.

All sorts of things can help here. Awards can play a part. Reviews. Your back story. A statement from you as the business owner setting out your principles and promises.

Ultimately, you need something that gives people a really strong reason as to why they should at least engage with you, even if they don't buy at this point.

Throw away your positioning, ignore it, or do it badly and you stack the odds against your marketing working whatever the media.

Personable and Relatable

This is another really key aspect of marketing that is missed by so many businesses that are in the lower parts of the pyramid.

Newsflash: people buy people.

One of the biggest advantages you have as a relatively small business over your big-business cousins is that it's a lot easier for you to be personable.

For that to happen, you have to start turning up in your marketing. Are you in it or on it? Literally.

You're the secret sauce in your business. You.

Are there photos and/or videos of you and your team?

That's what people are buying.

People relate to other people. Potential customers are looking for someone they can trust and when you're there, visible in your marketing, you make it easier for people to trust you and believe your message.

The additional challenge that you're giving yourself if you take a conscious decision not to be the face of your business is that it's much harder to build a business if you try and maintain a corporate façade when you're not one.

You're *(not yet)* the 300-pound marketing gorilla.

You're the wannabe trying to climb up that pyramid.

Your personality, visage and presence in your marketing is one of the best attributes you have to help you climb that pyramid. So don't throw it away because you're 'shy' or worried about what people might say. That would be really dumb and the price you'll pay will be huge in terms of reduced sales and profits.

There are examples all around of businesses who've used this really well. You know that people buy people.

If there's no photos or videos of you or your team on your website, you're missing a big trick.

Video

This is really simple.

No excuses. No inhibitions. It's time for you to embrace video.

What needs to be on your website are videos in which you and your team passionately educate your prospects.

Don't talk about yourself; talk about your customers and the situations that they're in. The problems you solve for them.

If you articulate the situation that your prospects are in, they'll come and talk to you.

Everyone else is talking about themselves and listing what they do. If you talk about the exact situation that you help people with on video, they're going to pick up the phone and talk to you. Promise.

They're seeing the real person with a nice short, succinct message that they can relate to.

Without it, you're making marketing so much harder for yourself.

Psst... want my team to create your video for you? Check out our Spotlight Videos service at: **spotlightvideos.co.uk**

Awards and Accreditations

If you've got it, flaunt it! Don't hide any lights under bushels. If you've got accreditations or awards of any sort, they need to be front and central.

Links to Independent Review Sites

This is becoming more and more important.

You want people to know that you're good at what you do – with a track record that proves it.

The best way to do that is to showcase the reviews and stars that you have on whichever site or sites are most relevant to what you do.

It might be Google, TripAdvisor, or Trustpilot, Facebook etc. Whatever is most relevant for your market.

This is absolutely essential for almost every business!

The world has changed in recent years. Independent review sites can add significant weight to your marketing and without it in your arsenal, you will miss out.

Testimonials

Testimonials are second best to reviews.

A testimonial isn't as good as reviews on independent sites, but they're useful nonetheless *(providing that they're properly displayed on your piece of collateral)*.

Properly displayed means that there's a photograph and real name of the person that you're quoting along with a unique headline that summarises the message.

The rule for your website is that you must have at least four testimonials for every year that you've been in business.

You won't get, for instance, 40 testimonials on a piece of printed collateral, *(if you've been around for 10 years, say)* but on your website you can. And you must.

Strong Offer *(with a deadline)*

Is there a reason to take action now?

This gets missed on so much marketing.

Of course not everybody will take action now, but that doesn't allow you as a business owner or marketer not to try. There'd better be a reason for them to take action now – with a deadline to do so.

Rigorously adding this element to all of your marketing will likely cause a dramatic uplift in response.

Our natural human state is to not do anything.

Take no action.

So when your marketing has no offer and no deadline, you're making it easy for people to 'wait till later' which means they'll do nothing because life will carry on.

It's really important that the reason to take action now has to be a real reason.

Multiple, Clear 'Calls to Action'

Have at least four, probably more!

It shouldn't be possible to scroll anywhere on your website and lose sight of a call-to-action link to click.

On your flyer or ad it should be crystal clear what you want them to do.

If a piece of marketing ticks all these 10 boxes, you're absolutely in the game!

But most marketing doesn't score particularly high, even though nothing that we've just told you is new.

It doesn't mean that everything grinds to a halt because you've got to redo everything. That's not what we're suggesting at all. Instead, when you do the Quality Test, you know where your weaknesses are.

As you go forward, you can start to do this work and make each piece of marketing better and more 'compliant' with the Quality Test.

This stuff really matters when it comes to moving markedly up the pyramid.

When you start to understand and enhance the quality of your collateral, it's like a multiplier effect.

When you have really high quality collateral you'll get more leads or enquiries and the quality of those enquiries tend to go up as well. It's a win-win.

But when you've got mediocre or poor-quality collateral, everything is harder.

2. Your Google My Business Listing

There are many businesses that are throwing away leads and enquiries *(and often the very highest calibre of leads and enquiries)*, because they haven't spent the two hours that it takes to sort out Google My Business properly.

It's not difficult to get access to your Google My Business listing and take control of it. And, broadly speaking, the more you put into your Google My Business listing, the more Google will reward you with more traffic and that normally equates to more leads and enquiries.

It's free - apart from the couple of hours of your time it will take to get it done properly.

Things to add include: your website *(and the link)*, company name, category, address, opening hours, descriptions of what you do.

You can also add posts, events that you've got coming up and offers to your Google My Business listing.

People can buy directly from Google My Business if you set it up properly.

They can sign up for newsletters. You can promote particular services at certain times.

If you set it up properly, they can message you from Google My Business.

If you put your number into Google My Business, they can ring you straight away.

More and more people are using it – and the profile that Google My Business listings get in the search results continues to grow.

It looks pretty certain that Google will continue to prioritise their Google My Business listings above so much of the organic traffic – which is another reason why you want to make sure you do it all properly.

You also want to put some photos and videos on Google My Business because, remember, people buy people.

The more stuff you have on Google My Business, the more leads and enquiries you'll get.

It's not difficult to do, it doesn't take much time. It hardly requires any technical knowledge.

If you're really stuck there's a complete how-to-guide in the Entrepreneurs Circle Vault. Members can login at **vault.entrepreneurscircle.org** & if you're not a member a member of Entrepreneurs Circle, you can join for free at: **entrepreneurscircle.org/join**

You just have to sort it out.

3. Your Follow-up Process

In any market, at any one time, there's a relatively small number of people who are looking to buy right now, today, this week. It's typically as low as 2% or 3%.

17% are going to buy fairly soon. They're in information-gathering mode.

20% know they've got a problem and will do something about it, but not in the immediate future.

60% of people aren't even aware that they've got a problem that needs your solution.

When you think about it, that means that 97% of your market isn't in the mode to buy now.

So you've got to make sure you keep in contact with them in the right way, over the right period of time so that when they're ready, they come to you.

One of the biggest pitfalls with so many people's marketing is that it's only screaming *"Buy our stuff now!"*.

But you know that 97% of people are not ready to buy now.

When all you're marketing is 'buy now', you're only appealing to a tiny fraction of potential buyers.

The really smart thing for the professional business person to do is use your marketing to attract people who may buy at some point and then keep in contact with them. Not in a 'salesy' way. You're not going to shout at them to buy every week, but you're going to find ways to help them and educate them.

The 50% who are kind of actively interested will have a look, watch a video, or perhaps download a cheat sheet if it's appropriately named and feels relevant to them. They love things like swipe files, short courses or webinars, for instance.

You can do a lot more with those people. You can attract them when you recognise that they're not going to buy straight away.

You can get their attention provided you've got the follow-up process in place.

But so many businesses haven't got systematic follow-up in place to nurture people over a prolonged period of time, yet it's a key element of the System.

As we've already discussed, the rhythmic acquisition of customers is always preceded by rhythmic activity.

One of those pieces of rhythmic activity is the regular communication with people who are in your funnel. People who aren't/weren't ready to buy now but will be in the future.

The professional business person never utters the words, *"My leads are crap"* or *"I'm unhappy with the quality of the leads."*

When you say that, you're letting other professional business people know that you're only focused on the 3% who are ready to buy now. It's very difficult to build a business with the rhythmic acquisition of customers when you're continually looking only for the people who are ready to buy now.

One of the biggest shifts you can make is to recognise that you want all the relevant people in your funnel. You're going to build a relationship with them through the personable, friendly, relatable messages that you send them. You'll make them smile. You'll inform and educate them.

You'll keep in touch with them over a prolonged period so that when they're ready to buy, they'll definitely, at least, talk to you.

That's what the professional business person does. That's what moves you up the pyramid.

Just because someone doesn't buy straight away doesn't make them a bad lead.

So systematically capture their contact information.

Then, utilise that contact information by systematically keeping in regular contact.

A few rules on the regular contact:

Use multiple media platforms, not just email. Do other things like send a text message, run Facebook ads just to people who are already on your list.

You're not going to try and sell all the time. What you're going to be all the time is useful and helpful.

You're going to make sure that all the communication that goes out comes from real people.
The language is right and appropriate and not full of corporate bollocks.

You're going to be personable and give of yourself. The more you give to people, the more you'll get back in terms of strength of relationship. If you tell them nothing about yourself, you keep them at arm's distance and it becomes much harder to pull them close. People like to know about your dog, children, family, or your holidays in the right way. *(People buy people, remember!)*

You'll also give content without any expectation of getting back.

This has been a big shift in the last two or three years. In a lot of ways, the re-marketing pixel is of more value to the professional marketer than an email address now because it's getting harder and harder to get attention in an inbox. But you can get attention on a Facebook page if you've got a pixel running through it.

They'll watch a 5 or 10-minute video and that's way more valuable than an email address. Because now they're getting to know you. They're investing time with you.

Now they pay attention to you and that moves them closer towards spending some money with you, which allows you to build your business.

Only occasionally do you ask them to buy. You should ask them for business, but not all the time. Not every week.

Now, to make all that happen, you need a CRM of some sort.

As the business owner, you'll need to own the systematic follow-up of all leads.

You can get help to do it, but you have to own it. It's too important to your place on the pyramid to hand-it off completely.

The frequency of days that you would send your first 10 follow-up messages out should be something like this:

- On day zero *(the day the lead came in)*, you're going to deliver what they've asked for.

They've asked for something – that's why they've given you their details.

- On the following day, you make sure they've got it in a nice, friendly, personal helpful way as if you typed it yourself.

- The second email that day, you'll write that you were thinking about them earlier and thought they might find this helpful as well. If you do it well, it feels really personable.

- The following day, you'll ask how they're getting on with that stuff you sent them.

Is it worth having a chat?

Don't fluff it up. It's only one line. Now you're taking an interest in them and you're being personable and relatable.

- The following day, you'll ask if they knew about all your services and mention something that you do as well.

- Then you get a day off.

- On day five, you mention that you can help with x, y and z and ask if it's worth setting up a call.

- On day eight, you tell them a story about someone like them that you've helped.

- On day 13, you mention that if they've got this problem or you need this, here's an offer, with a deadline.

- On day 21, you mention that it's been a little while since they enquired. You're sure you could help and ask them to let you know when would be a good time to call.

- On day 34, if you haven't heard from them, you ask if you've upset them.

You've sent them all this stuff, but they've not come back to you.

You're really sorry if you've upset or offended them and ask what you could do to make it right.

These are emails that everybody could put in place that would catapult them into the top 1% in their market.

Systematically start to follow up all those precious leads that you're paying cash, time and money for!

4. Remarketing and Pixel Tracking

Pixel tracking and remarketing is a big deal.

Remarketing is really valuable for brand building and getting your name out there. The professional business person is definitely doing it.

If you're not familiar with what it is, remarketing is when you put some code on your website, one from Google and one from Facebook. It then allows you to show people who've been to your website messages, adverts, and banners, when they're doing other stuff around the Internet.

You'll have noticed it yourself, I'm sure, when you've been to a website and then, later, when you're browsing other sites you start seeing ads for the exact business that you were looking at previously. That's remarketing in action and it's a very powerful tool.

All the businesses at the top of the pyramid are using it – and you should be too.

It's a really useful way to generate leads and also nurture those leads.

One thing we've found is that our conversion rates on remarketing increase over time.

We've found that we get a higher response the longer we've been showing remarketing messages to people.

We get more people responding on our ads in week three and month two than we do on day two or day three.

The more often they see it, the more likely they are to respond, which is slightly counter-intuitive.

It all plays into what you're doing in terms of becoming a feature in people's lives.

Remarketing clicks are usually the cheapest clicks available.

Google also has Remarketing Lists for Search Ads *(RLSA)* which is when you're showing remarketing ads to people who've searched for what you do but haven't yet been to your website. You're remarketing to them based on what they've searched, not just what they've done, which is a brilliant way to hone and target the right audience.

It combines what Google called the intent of the search query with context. So, you can show remarketing ads to people who haven't even been to your website, if you do it properly. It's really powerful when you know what you're doing.

If you haven't got the pixel tracking code on your website and you're not engaged in this, you can't do it. You're completely hamstrung. You've thrown away a really useful marketing pillar.

Though it will be a fairly small percentage of your remarketing pool that will convert, they are usually very cost-effective conversions for most businesses.

Not running remarketing would be dumb.

There's no way the professional business person would not have remarketing running on their site and be doing it properly.

Most people do it in a very simplistic way.

Most people run remarketing and show the same ads to all visitors who've been to their website in the last 30 days. Now, just to be clear, that's way better than not doing it at all, but it's not the smartest approach. It's fairly unsophisticated.

If you're going to do remarketing, it isn't difficult to do it much smarter than that.

You just do a little grid. It's so simple. It's a little 12-boxed grid with basically two axis.

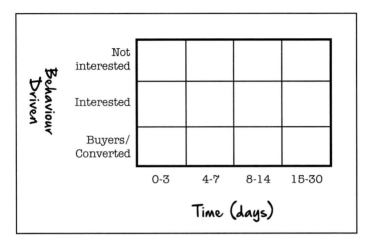

The left-hand axis measures the behaviour. People really fall into three categories on most websites.

How do you know who came to your website and were interested as opposed to who came to your website and weren't interested?

It's really straightforward. You just look at the data and numbers. Like so many things in this system, it's all in the numbers.

The people who aren't interested will be the people who came to one page and left. In other words, your bounce rate.

The people who came to one page and left are probably not interested. It's probably not worth spending money remarketing to those people.

People who came on to your site, though, and visited two-four pages are probably quite interested.

So, at a very simple level, split it into three:

First Level: Not interested.
People who came to one page and bounced straight off.

Second Level: Interested.
People who went to more than one page.

Third Level: Converted.
People who converted or did what you wanted them to do. They filled in the form and got the download.

That's the three types of behaviour.

Then, you'll look at the time since their visit:
0–3 days; 4–7 days; 8–14 days; 15–30 days.

You then do your remarketing.

So, you wouldn't spend any money on the people who aren't interested. You don't run any remarketing ads to them whatsoever.

You'll put most of your budget in the first three days on the people who are interested.

You'll reduce that budget over time because the chance of them doing something will get less over time.

All those people who convert, you take that straight into a Google mix to find a similar audience and you start showing ads to a similar audience, people who Google know share the same characteristics as the people who did what you wanted them to do.

None of that is difficult to do. It's not complex.

It's not challenging.

Once this stuff settles, it can sit and run typically for quite a long time.

You don't need to go and tinker and tweak. You want to have a look at it once a month and see your stats. Put some sensible budget on it.

The numbers and cost per click are small, but you'll start to build your brand, presence and lead flow.

It's a really important Foundation Block.

You're going to be spending relatively modest sums to get clicks or leads through your remarketing, but without it you're missing out on what are quite high-value leads when they start to come through.

You can't skip remarketing. It's an integral part of the System and it would be absolutely foolish of you not to do it.

In fact, we can't think of a scenario when a business wouldn't want to do remarketing.

These are people who are coming to your website. You want to maintain messaging them in the days and weeks after they've been to your site.

It also gives you a massive competitive edge because, again, most of your competitors aren't doing this stuff. They're not visible to this extent.

They're very primitive in their marketing approach. They're largely ignorant. So, you have a significant opportunity to get ahead of the game here. This stuff normally ends up paying for itself really quickly.

5. Your Price Review

This is an interesting one.

So many businesses have such a lot of opportunities to add a five-figure sum to their net profit.

All you have to do is put your prices up by 10%.

Just put your average price up by 10% and look at what happens to your profitability – it's ten grand plus, even in a relatively small business.

It can be a silver bullet to growing your profitability and moving you up the pyramid.

There's a lot of businesses that haven't properly reviewed their pricing for quite some time and we often uncover some quite big opportunities here.

This is the one Foundation Block which can literally at a stroke move a business markedly forward in terms of profitability.

The price all of us charge is down to us as the business owners.

But what we decide on price and how we present our price affects a lot of things in business.

It affects how we're seen and our positioning in the marketplace.

If you're positioned at a low price, it comes with implications. The price you charge affects the calibre of staff that you can bring into your business. You can only afford lower-priced staff if you've got lower-priced products and services.

It affects the kind of customers you attract.

It impacts the pride you feel in your business as well to a large extent and, of course, it also impacts your profits.

There's a lot at play when it comes to price, yet it isn't something that people think about sufficiently enough.

Your profit is power.

When you have a business that's chucking out all the profit you need, it allows you to do all the things you want to do.

This means you get to choose the prosperity you want in your life by the choice you make about price.

I'm not suggesting that you act completely in a vacuum, but with the right thinking, price can take you into very different places.

We learned a long time ago that: *"You can go to the ocean with a teaspoon or a bucket. The ocean doesn't care."*

Think of the ocean as all the money that's out there in the world.

You can take a little tiny bit or you can take a big glob.

The ocean doesn't care.

There's plenty to go around.

The prices that you charge are your choice and your responsibility.

Here's another way to think about it: is the service you provide pretty average?

Most people will say: *"No. We provide a really great service. We look after our customers really well. We care about them in a way that our competitors really don't."*

Well, if that's the case, why are you only charging an average price?

It becomes much harder to provide an above-average service if you have an average or below-average price because you haven't got the money in the business to invest in the right way, on the right things.

One of the reasons why it's expensive to go to Disney is because they charge a lot to get in.

That's for two reasons:

1. It's very profitable as a business, but also because it means they can create an experience that's way above average.

And...

2. Because it's way above average, people want to go back again and tell other people.

If Disney charged $10 a day to get in, instead of $110, the experience would be very different. It wouldn't be as good and, therefore, people wouldn't come.

All this links back to pricing strategies.

Walt Disney always had an eye on the angle. It was Walt who determined that all rides must end in a gift shop.

What it means is the average spend of their visitors goes up. You've obviously bought your ticket, but then you buy the additional extras and you can't just walk straight out of the gift shop because they've made it really hard to see the door. You have to meander around to get out. That's an angle.

The money comes in to support all the attractions and the investment that's there.

People fail at price for a number of reasons.

Many are ignorant because they just don't realise what they could do.

They think their market won't do stuff or they're frightened of the implications if they increase prices.

Here's a good example:

Some years ago, my wife bought me a voucher package for some personal training sessions for Christmas. I'm a very busy guy and I hate going to the gym. She thought this guy could come to the office and train me.

He came one day to see me and I said: *"This is only going to work if you can come on my time."*

He said: *"Yeah, I'll be very flexible."*

I said: *"I'd like you to come at 6:30 on Monday."*

"Sorry, I can't. I've got someone that comes at 6:30 on Monday."

"Okay. How about 7:00am on Tuesday?"

"Sorry, I can't do 7:00 on Tuesday."

Basically he couldn't fit me in.

I get chatting to this guy and realised that he's very busy as a personal trainer, but he was charging only £25 an hour.

The guy's full. He's got no capacity and he's working all hours.

He's working really hard, and he's a nice guy.

His wife is quite a good salesperson and she's quite successful. She just won an award and, as a result, she was taking him to Barbados on holiday, which he felt kind of emasculated about.

He felt it should be him taking her. But she was taking him.

I then discover that he has this goal to open up his own gym.

It became really clear to me what he needed to do. I said, *"You need to double your prices."* After all he was full with people paying him a low price.

He said, *"If I double my prices, I'll lose half my customers."*

Of course, that's exactly the right thing to do.
That's exactly the point!

It means he would have the same income coming in and half his week left to fill with other people who are paying twice the price. So, he would end up with a business that's twice as profitable.

But he couldn't get it.

He was massively restricted, because he really felt he couldn't do it.

Five years on he's still busy with people paying him way less than he's worth. He's failing at price. He hasn't understood. And he's way down the bottom of the pyramid.

People fail at price because they make mistakes with their marketing and their selling.

Price can be a very positive marketing tool. Reassuringly expensive is quite a good thing in some instances.

You have a responsibility as a business owner, especially if you have things that you want to achieve, to make sure that you create the greatest possible profit you can in your business.

The choices you make on price can inhibit that.

Business maths says that there has to be enough money to do what needs to be done.

So, the most amazing marketing in the world can't overcome poor business maths.

There's got to be enough!

Part of business maths is the price that you're charging.

One of the biggest challenges is that people handicap themselves with bare bones pricing.

As a result, you haven't got enough money to market and promote yourself properly.

You haven't got enough money to wow your customers after the sale because you can't do the things you want to do because your margins are so tight.

You can't hire the best staff so you make do with mediocre staff. That results in mediocre service.

You've got no money to differentiate your offering.

You can drive sales with bare bones pricing, but it's very difficult to sustain a successful business with bare bones pricing.

You need the money to do all the other stuff.

Another area that causes people to fail on price is using textbook formulas or industry norms to set their price.

There's no reason why you have to do that. You can think differently about it.

In our experience, people are excessively concerned about their competitor's prices when really they're not in the same market. If you market yourself properly, you can extract yourself from that. When you go low on price, you can attract customers who buy on price and that can be a recipe for failure in the medium term.

The trick is to present your product to the market in a way that makes it impossible to compare it to others. So, you create features and elements about your products that others can't have because that gives you a lever to sort the pricing out.

Not offering premium price options is another biggie.

One of the first questions we ask people when we're working with them as their Coach is what's the most money I could spend with you.

If I think you're great, how much can I spend?

A lot of businesses haven't got that upward spread at the top end of their range.

Introducing the right premium price options can make a big difference.

Only a small percentage of your customers will take it. It's not about putting the price up for everybody, but it's giving people somewhere to go so they can get the better version dressed up in whatever way you want to do it.

Again, it can be a really easy fix.

I want you to picture the scene.

At one of my Inner Circle meetings, we were going through what each member wanted to achieve in the year. This particular guy said: *"This is the year I get real. I get serious. I need to generate £160,000 of top line growth this year."*

He explained why that was the case, and how a lot of that top line growth would flow down to the bottom line because his costs are fairly fixed.

I said: *"How many customers have you got?"*

He has a business that people pay monthly with over 2,000 existing customers. They're paying relatively small sums: £20 – £25 per month.

"When did you last put your price up?", we asked next.

He was embarassed and admitted that he hadn't put any prices up for over 8 years!

So I dictated a very short letter to all his customers that basically said that their price hadn't gone up since the London Olympics and it was going up by £6 a month starting next month.

Bless him. He sent the letter.

Of course, the guy was scared that he'd lose customers – and he did. He lost 4 customers – out of more than 2,000.

The loss of £110 per month from the four that left was more than compensated for by the extra £12,500 he banked from all those who stayed. Voila! - he basically achieved his £160,000 uplift in what was less than five minutes because he thought differently about price.

Having had the realisation, he then had the balls to go through and execute it and his business was changed markedly as a result.

His was one of the quickest surges up the pyramid ever – but it would never have happened if he hadn't been part of the coaching group.

Sometimes we need help to see what's right in front of our face. An external perspective can make a huge difference.

If you're going to implement the Entrepreneurs Marketing and Sales System yourself without any help, you need to review your pricing properly and look honestly at what you've got and done.

Another price failure is the issue of poor self-esteem.

A lot of people, more than you realise, don't feel worthy in some way.

The ultimate failure on price is when people struggle forever, when they settle for less; when they give up on ambition because of inadequate thinking.

The million-pound secret: low cost and cheap have concealed costs and when you reveal those concealed costs to the market, there are customers who are unwilling to incur those concealed costs. They prefer to pay money.

Everything's got a concealed cost.

For example, one of the concealed cost of cheap furniture is that you have to replace it sooner. It's your job to educate your market as to the concealed costs.

Recognise that you're in control of your pricing.

You can decide what you want to do.

Get conscious of the business maths and then test it.

You don't have to put your price up for everybody. Just try selling it at a bit higher price. See what happens.

Take a bravery pill and then implement.

6. Your Systemised Review Collection

We're living in a society which is obviously much more digitally savvy than ever before.

You might not believe this, but in July 2005, I announced what was the first publicly available review system on a website anywhere in the UK.

Even Amazon wasn't doing reviews properly back then. There was no Trustpilot or TripAdvisor.

It's the most normal thing now to be able to leave reviews online, but it wasn't back in the summer of 2005.

There's tons of data that show how important reviews are to consumers now. In short, reviews matter.

Different platforms matter more to different industries, but there are a handful that matter more than others. Obviously, if you're in hospitality, TripAdvisor is where it's at.

If you're in business with an aspiration to build something successful and sustainable, you need the systemised collection of reviews. Only amateurs would leave it to chance.

At the moment, why don't your customers leave you lots of reviews online?

The answer: they never think to do so.

It's not that they hate you. It's not that they don't value what you do. It's just that they're never reminded to go and leave a review online.

This can be really frustrating as a business owner. Except, there's no excuse if you're a professional business owner in not getting this fixed.

Here's an example of the sort of system we're talking about:
An estate agent sells a house.

The vendor receives an email from the MD of the agency the day after they sold the house. It says something like:

"Delighted that we sold the house for you yesterday. Can you just tell us how did our guy in York do? How would you rate the service that you got out of 10?"

So, people who said 9 or 10 got a second email.

It was sent two or three hours later.

It would say something like:

"Hi Noel, fantastic that Bob in York did such a good job for you.

Bob would love it if you could click the link below and leave a short review on this Trustpilot site, because that puts fuel in his tank.

He'd really appreciate that little gesture, if you're able to do so.

Thanks ever so much."

If you'd scored it less than 9, you got a different email.

That email would say:

"Noel, thank you for your feedback.

I'm really sorry to hear that we didn't wildly excite you with the service that you got from our guys in York.

Can you tell me what we could've done differently that would've made it better for you?"

If they ranked five or lower, they rang them up and dealt with the problem straight away.

The end result is that estate agency started to get loads of five-star reviews, because the people who were asked to leave the reviews were the people who they knew were happy.

They didn't get any bad reviews, because all the people who rated them low on that initial email were followed up personally.

They went out of their way to make good whatever the problem was.

You can have that system in your business.

It's delivered by a product called Grade.us. There are similar ones around, but that's the best service by a mile.

What Grade.us does is exactly what I've just described. You can have it in your business. It will take you, roughly speaking, 45 minutes to set up.

It will help you to get reviews and monitor them.

It will help you to amplify all the good reviews that you get by sharing them on your social feeds, website, etc.

The tools they have are just fantastic! It sends out a similar email asking people to tell you what they think about your service. You set the triggers. You can define all that and put it in the system, or you can do it manually.

The responses that scored the estate agent 9 or 10 kicks off a certain sequence to get reviews. Those that put a lower score in come back another way, giving you the chance to fix the relationship with people.

You can then put those reviews directly onto the platforms that matter most to you.

You can send it by email and you can send them a little text reminder as well. It's all automated in the system once it's set up. It takes feeds out of your CRM, if it's done properly.

Once the reviews are added, Grade.us can stream them into your website.

So, you're seeing the constant stream.

You get reports every month that tell you what's happening too.

You get alerts from people who've scored you low so you can contact them and follow through, effectively cutting them off before they start venting on social media, or on review sites.

You find out that they're unhappy, and then you can take action if you put the system in place.

It's that regular flow of reviews that builds people's confidence and trust in you.

Having a bunch of five-star reviews is great, but what's much more useful is having a flow. So, every week there's new ones being added. That's what makes it real.

What you do then, if you're sensible, is you start to respond to the reviews on the platforms as well. This would be a weekly task for someone in the business.

Set up the automated campaign so that you can get that rhythmic flow of reviews coming in. That flow gives people confidence to buy from you. They're seeing what other people are saying about you.

> **DEAL:** readers of this book can get the Grade.us review platform for just £49/month *(rather than £149/month!)* at: **EMSSystem.co.uk/reviews**

7. Your Marketing Calendar

Back in the 1990s, the Chief Exec at Barclays took a decision which was groundbreaking at the time. He brought a guy called Malcolm Hewitt, an 'ousider', a retail expert, into Barclays to run the UK branch network.

My job was to orient Malcolm into the business, because I knew the branch network.

One of the things that Malcolm did, which was genius, was to put in place a Marketing Calendar for all the branches.

There were eight slots each year in Barclays' Marketing Calendar and the Product Managers had to bid for those slots.

Hewitt mobilised the entire network for a six or seven week window behind a certain product.

For example, in spring they'd have mortgages. Now, you could still buy a mortgage the rest of the year, but all the focus was on mortgages for six weeks in spring.

Car registrations used to change in August. So, in the run up to August it was car loans.

There was a focus on certain things at certain times of the year and it brought about two huge impacts.

The first was focus. Everyone was focused on a particular product/ campaign at any one time.

And the result of that focus was significant.

Malcolm talked about the need, when you wanted to drive sales, to lead the market.

Don't react; lead it.
We're not suggesting that you have eight campaigns a year, but we are suggesting that you might want to have two or three. There's at least two, probably three, campaigns in every business.

There are things that you can create that give you a reason to go to market. You can create some noise about it. Get people talking. It's what we do at Entrepreneurs Circle. We have a Marketing Calendar with four or five campaigns each year. Each campaign is planned and scheduled in advance. All running for a limited time. All with an offer. And a deadline.

You can do the same.

Get creative. You can engage your team. Get out there and lead your market.

This is you as a professional business owner, recognising that there are a number of times in the year when you can mobilise and get a campaign in place.

Without a Marketing Calendar, it doesn't get thought about until it's typically too late.

It's not the most dramatic of the 11 Foundation Blocks but it can make a very meaningful contribution when it's done properly.

8. Your Knowledge Centre

This is driven by an amazing book written by Marcus Sheridan called *'They Ask, You Answer'*.

The whole premise of this book *(and it's more than a premise because it's proven and it works)* is to set out to passionately educate your prospects.

When you do it properly, amazing things can happen.

It's an easy read, but its impact can be startling.

The bit that people often miss is the *'passionately educating'*.

It's a minimum of one piece of content each week, which might feel like a bit of an arduous task. But each article is an answer to a real question that real potential customers ask. You know this stuff anyway. It's the questions that you answer week in and week out anyway.

The best and easiest way to do it is to record the answers on video.

You can then put the videos up on your site. You can put them on YouTube to get more traffic and then you can transcribe the videos into a blog article as well.

Make sure you name the pages. Every article sits on a separate page because you want to make it really easy for Google to find the pages.

The title of the page is exactly the question that you're answering, because that's how Google knows to give your page as the search result when people are searching for that 'thing', which you know people are searching for because you've done the research properly.

You'll realise that just by answering the questions that people are asking, you can start to fulfil your goals as well.

Now it's really important to say at this point: please read the book yourself. Don't rely on this 200 word summary of it. Buy it, read it, study it. It will serve you so well.

Of course, most people won't do this because it feels like a lot of work. And business owners in general are not good at doing the hard work that makes the selling easy.

But this isn't really a lot of work once you get your head in the right place, because you answer the questions anyway every day, or every week. All you've got to do is answer them on a video camera, and then get it transcribed.

Rev.com will sort your transcription brilliantly. It's a super quick service and very cost effective.

Consumers aren't dumb.

Expectations have changed.

People who help people get more business but most businesses don't embrace this 'teacher mentality' online.

Come at this from your potential customers' perspective.

What do they want to know?

Tell them, answer them, and passionately educate them...

The best topics to cover are pricing and costs, problems that people have, comparisons of different products or options and *(honest)* reviews of different products.
By the way, you can involve your whole team.

This isn't just your job as the business owner. If you've got people who talk with your customers and can come up with answers, use 'em.

9. Your Neighbourhood Cards

Foundation Block number nine is your Neighbourhood Cards *(if appropriate)*.

If you don't go to your customers' or clients' places of work, you will not need this. You can skip straight on...

If you do go out to your customers' homes or business when you deliver your product or service, this is an important part of your marketing foundations.

It's a really simple thing.

When you go to somebody's house, you drop cards through the letterbox of five houses to the left, five to the right and five – ten to the homes opposite.

Here's an example of the wording on a typical Neighbourhood Card:

"Hello! You might have seen our van in the street.

We're working at Jess and Dave's at number seven. Feel free to pop by if you have any questions about anything electrical, no matter how big or small.

You never know when you might need us, so stick this card to your fridge."

It's an implicit endorsement.

When you start to drop those cards, you'll be amazed at how many people start to ring you up.

For relatively little effort, all of a sudden your phone is starting to ring and you're getting leads coming in. It's almost like a preemptive referral.

The trick is to systemise the distribution of the cards: five either side and five opposite on each and every job. No exceptions.

The job's not complete until the cards have been dropped. That's the challenge.

10. Your Use of LinkedIn

If you're B2B you MUST to do this.

FACT: some of your potential customers will go and look you up on LinkedIn.

LinkedIn's usage is going up rapidly. People will look for you on LinkedIn. So you want to make sure that when they find you on LinkedIn, it says the right things.

This is a Foundation Block that you do once and then you can almost forget about it.

Sort what I do, how I do it, who I work with, what people are saying, my background, contact me, and your profile is done.

The good news is it'll be a relatively quick one to tick off for most people.

Even if you're not proactively using LinkedIn yourself, fix your profile because you never know who's going on there to look you up.

Now, of course, LinkedIn can also be a rich source of new leads and new business but that side of things is a little different to *'sorting-your-profile-properly'* which is what this Foundation Block is all about.

11. Answering Your Phone

The last, but by no means least, Foundation Block is answering the phone.

No one intends to miss a call. We understand that but every day, in tens of thousands of businesses, including potentially yours, people are missing calls.

Calls get missed for three main reasons:

1. Blissful Ignorance
(There's no alert or alarm to tell the business owner that they missed a phone call.)

2. Inadequate Systems
   (Sometimes that can be because there's not enough phone lines or extensions – so the poor customer gets an engaged tone and you never knew they were trying to ring.)
3. Not Enough People Answering
   (The customer gets a ringing tone but no one picks up.)

You'd be amazed the number of times this happens.

Staggered. Stunned.

It's just a Foundation Block. It's not going to catapult you forward.

But it's a basic fundamental of business.

You wouldn't run a shop and not be open on a Saturday morning.

Why would you run a business with a phone number that doesn't get answered at core working hours during the week?

Some people, on some occasions, are going to ring you up. There'll be occasions when you aren't able to deal with that yourself.

So, why would you not put in place an overflow and look at it as a marketing cost?

You can't profess to be a professional business person until you've got that bit boxed off somehow.

There are plenty of call handling companies who can do a great job for you.

In the EC office, the phone rings three times and if it's not picked up it diverts straight to the call handling service at Office Genies *(Give 'em a call on 01604 532 022, we can highly recommend them)*. It means we literally never miss a call.

Oh, and don't kid yourself that you've got a voicemail or answering machine so people will leave a message. Which decade are you in? That might have been OK in the '90s but most people don't/won't leave a message these days and your potential new customers, who you've spent money and effort marketing to, won't hang around. They'll be dialling the next company on their list. You'll lose their business and you'll never know how close you came to getting it.

If only you'd answered the bloody phone!

> *You can download resources for all of these foundation blocks at:*
> **https://EMSSystem.co.uk/downloads**

CHAPTER SEVEN:
THE MARKETING

*"Good marketing makes
the business look smart.*

*Great marketing makes
the customer feel smart"*

Joe Chernov

So, you've worked through the first two parts of the System.

You have a plan, you know your numbers, and your Foundations Blocks are in place.

If you've followed the System so far you'll also have a high level of consciousness about your personal reason why you want to implement the System.

The big return from the System comes from fixing your marketing.

To crack the rhythmic acquisition of customers you somehow have to attract not just anybody, but the right people.

You then have to educate them not just in terms of why they might want to do business with you, but also, in some instances, you have to educate people about the problems they have and why they need the solutions that you have.

So you have to attract them.

And you have to educate them.

Most will not be ready to buy now. Get your head round that. That's one of the fundamentals.

There's a reason why you require a marketing and sales system in your business: it's because only a tiny portion of your market is ready to buy right now.

Once you have their interest and you've attracted them, in some way you need to nurture that relationship. One of the biggest gaps that most people have is a huge inadequacy to nurture prospects or leads.

You have to attract the right people, make sure they understand what you do, why you do it, and, most importantly, why you're right for them. Then, nurture that relationship by keeping in touch so that when they're ready to buy, it's you that they come to.

So with all that in mind... lets get stuck in.

At the moment, the reason why the vast majority of those thousands of potential customers of yours aren't buying from you is because they don't know about you.

They haven't looked at you and considered you.

They haven't consciously decided not to buy from you.

They either don't know about you or they've forgotten about you.

They maybe knew about you once.

They might have got something from you six weeks ago, but they weren't ready to buy at that point. And their lives are busy.

*(**IMPORTANT:** Everyone's life is busy – there's no one sitting round waiting and hoping that you're going to send them some marketing today!)*

When it came to making the buying decision, you weren't anywhere near the top of their mind. That's why they bought from someone else.

It's not because you're rubbish at what you do. The opposite is true in the vast majority of cases.

It's not because you haven't done some marketing, because you have.

But what you've failed to do is nurture your relationship with these people.

So, in short, not enough people know about you and what you do – and most of those that do have forgotten about you when it comes to them making a buying decision. Not a very cheery situation is it!

But don't despair. This is normal for businesses in the middle or bottom of the pyramid. And it's not that hard to fix.

You will start by defining a specific outcome. The more specific the better.

So, if you run an optician's practice, your defined outcome would be X number of eye tests per week, with an average spend of £Y.

If your running a restaurant, your defined outcome would be X number of covers per night/week at an average spend of £Y.

If you're an IFA, it might be X new funds under management.

If you're a will writer, it would be X number of new wills written this week.

If you're a photographer, your defined outcome would be X number of shoots per week at an average spend of £Y.

You get the idea.

With all these examples, if the defined outcomes above are achieved, the business will do OK and reach it goals. And by simplifying the defined outcome into just one or two key measures, it gets focus and can be understood by everybody in the business.

Everything is about making sure we hit the defined outcomes this week...

It's powerful stuff.

So you're going to define a very specific outcome that you want to get.

It may take time to get your defined outcome defined right.

In fact, it's one of the main areas where we typically focus with our Coaching Client because it isn't always easy. You MUST have a good grasp of your numbers in order to define the right outcome and, of course, a clear understanding of what you're trying to achieve - i.e where you want to be.

Your defined outcome will help you get there.

Armed with a well defined outcome we can then start to take action to make it happen.

So, let's say we're running an optician's practice and we need 50 eye tests per week.

We have a database of past customers so we're going to get proactive at ringing them up and booking them in one or two weeks in advance *(we won't rely on the old-fashioned sending of reminder cards. That's so 1990s and the phone call will be way more effective – and cheaper – at getting a high proportion booked in. It also helps us to build relationships by talking with them).*

Let's say we think 35 of the slots each week can be filled from our existing customers by phoning them up and sending cards in the post to those that we can't get hold of. It becomes someone's responsibility in the business to make those calls, send those cards and deliver a defined outcome of 35 eye tests per week.

That leaves us with another 15 eye tests to fill – and we'll need new customers in order to do it.

We decide to run Google Ads, highly targeted to our local area so we capture people who are actively looking. We think Google will bring us one or two eye tests a week.

We decide to run an ad in a local community magazine and we expect to get one eye test per week from that.

Then we pin big hopes on a Facebook campaign with an aspiration of 8-10 eye tests per week from that.

The Marketing

Next on our plan might be an initiative with a large local employer to get their staff in for tests. This could be worth 2-3 tests per week

For each of these marketing pillars, we need to create the marketing asset i.e the ad.

So we define the outcome and then create the asset.

Then, you start to run the marketing.

You put it out there into the world to see if you can get the response that you want.

As you have a specific outcome in mind, you know where you need it to go.

Next, you must track the numbers. This is the bit where most people go wrong.

You look at everything that's happened. You're not just looking at how many customers have booked an eye test immediately from this. You're looking at everything around it.

The fifth step is to review what your numbers tell you and adjust your plan.

And you repeat this five-step process:
1. Define the Outcome
2. Compile Your Plan
3. Create the Marketing Asset
4. Get it out there and Test
5. Review Results and Adjust...

To sum up, you must know what it is that you're trying to achieve from each initiative or campaign.

Once you have the specific outcome, you create the asset.

Then, you test it at a small scale with a low spend, track the numbers, review and repeat.

This little five-step cycle will be happening lots of times across your marketing system.

It's not a difficult thing to do. It's not time-consuming. But it makes a real big difference when it's executed properly.

If you can just start to do one a week or one a fortnight or one a month.

This is how you'll put the System in place over time.

This approach is going to be fundamental to you cracking the rhythmic acquisition of customers. Without a little five-step system like this, you'll never get there, because random activity can never lead to predictable things happening.

Some things that you do won't work. This is to be expected. This is the nature of what we do as marketers. Nobody gets everything right all the time.

Fundamentally, there will be one of two reasons why a marketing campaign won't work for you.

Sometimes the reason you didn't get the result in the campaign was because you executed it poorly. It ain't what you do. It's the way that you do it, that's what gets results.

It might have been the way the copy was written. It might have been the way you followed up. It can be very helpful to get a third-party perspective on it.

There's a second reason why things won't work. We call it market feedback or response.

What you're taking to market isn't sufficiently attractive for them. Your *'offer'* wasn't good enough. The marketing worked insofar as they got your message but the market didn't like what you had for them. That's why they didn't respond.

Sometimes you take stuff to the market and you're really passionate about it. You really believe in it. You've put so much work and effort into it. Sometimes the market, though, doesn't want what you're selling.

Especially in the early days of developing a business or campaign, you have to be very mindful of this.

A lot of marketing fails because the *'offer'* was just not good enough.

All your prospects are being bombarded every day with commercial messages from thousands of other businesses all wanting their time and attention.

You have to stand out if you're going to get a look in.

It's very important how you discern and handle the setbacks and disappointing results. It will be key to your ultimate success.

Because you are going to have big setbacks.

You're going to get onto something that you were convinced was the winner, and it's going to fall flat on its face.

It's difficult when that happens. The hardest thing is to think sufficiently clearly to be able to discern the real reasons why.

Your ability to discern accurately makes a huge difference in business – and again it's where an experienced Coach or third party can play a big part.

Enjoying the book?

*Properly implement the EMS System with the full video training programme at **EMSSystem.co.uk/video***

CHAPTER EIGHT:
THE PITFALLS

"It's clear the future holds great opportunities. It also holds pitfalls. The trick will be to avoid the pitfalls, seize the opportunities, and get back home by six o'clock."

Woody Allen

There are a number of big 'bear-traps' waiting to catch the amateur marketer and business owner.

The first pitfall is **not asking people to buy often enough.**

There's a lot of reasons for that. Most commonly, the business owner gets worried about being seen as too 'salesy'. Don't. The price you pay for that is really high. It's not hard to make offers without sounding 'salesy' when you know how.

The second common pitfall is **ignoring the mindset side of marketing and selling.** You see, your customers aren't you – and you are not your customer.

Not everyone in the world thinks like you do.
(We know they should – but they don't!)

Your customers don't obsess about your business.

They're living their own lives. They're focused on their own challenges and problems.

The third pitfall is that **you can't be boring. Ever**.

Somehow, you have to get people's attention and you won't accomplish that by being bland and beige and the same as everyone else. Like everyone else does!

The next pitfall when it comes to fixing your marketing is **getting stuck in the weeds.**

You're always doing, and never marketing.

It starts insidiously.

Or else you get on the Marketing Rollercoaster.

You know the one. When you do some marketing and get some new customers and then you're too busy looking after those customers so you don't do any marketing and then the customers dry up so you do some marketing again. Up and down on the 'coaster'. Famine to feast and back to famine again.

It's very difficult to hand all your marketing off to an employee. You need to at least own and be responsible for making sure the right things are happening. You can get help to do it, but you have to be the one overseeing.

If you get stuck in the weeds, recognise that the marketing system ain't going to work.

And if the marketing system doesn't work, those plans and goals that you had are sailing away over the horizon.

You have to get out of the weeds.

Pitfall number five is **forgetting the business maths.**

When you do the maths properly and accurately, it's nearly always easy to make the right decisions – confidently.

If you do the maths wrong – or the wrong maths - it can lead you to really bad decisions. Stupid even.

The sixth pitfall is a **poor decision-making process.**

What we mean by that is decisions about marketing that are taken almost instinctively. That's rarely a good thing. The numbers should shape *(almost)* all decisions about your marketing.

What's the defined outcome?

You've created this asset. You've run a test. These are the numbers from the test. Now review the numbers, do the maths, and that will take you to the right decision in almost every case.

If you decide to stop doing Facebook Ads, for instance, you have to recognise that for a lot of businesses you've just chopped off your right leg.

And if your business goal is the equivalent of walking up Snowdon then you chop off your right leg, that is a really dumb thing to do.

Because for lots of businesses, your market is on Facebook. That's where you can find 'em and communicate with them.

Without it, it's much harder to do either of those things.

It's not impossible to get to where you want to get to, but when you amputate limbs you make mobility much harder.

So, you need to think really clearly, if you're making the decision to stop doing Facebook Ads, for instance. And no professional business owner would ever make a decision like that based on a single test.

The asset you created could be the problem.

The creativity of the ad could be the problem.

The problem could be in the offer that you made.

It could be in the audience that you selected.

There are all sorts of variables in the mix that could be the reason why that particular test failed.

There aren't many situations where we haven't been able to make Facebook Ads work.

Many people in business approach marketing by trying one thing at random. It doesn't work and they condemn themselves never to do it again.

It's really stupid, but that's how most people approach marketing because their decision making process is flawed.

Pitfall number seven is **insufficient follow-up.**

Your follow-up is really key – as we've already discussed.

And the final pitfall to watch out for is if **all your marketing is screaming 'buy our stuff'** because then you're only appealing to a very small fraction of your potential buyers.

In your market not everybody is ready to buy right now. Be very mindful of that.

CHAPTER NINE:
THE PARTHENON

"Earth proudly wears the Parthenon as the best gem upon her zone"

Ralph Waldo Emerson

The Parthenon is a remarkable structure.

It was built over 2400 years ago, and it's still standing.

The reason why it's still standing is because of all those pillars.

Even if it lost two or three of those pillars, it isn't going to fall down because there are plenty of pillars that keep its roof structure in place.

In a lot of businesses, there aren't many pillars.

Most businesses haven't even got four pillars, and so they couldn't even keep a simple roof up at all.

When you ain't got many pillars, your roof is very exposed if something happens with one particular pillar.

In terms of putting in place a marketing and sales system, having multiple pillars is really smart.

So, that's what you're going to work towards.

You don't have to build them all at once.

You have time to build them in the right way.

You'll define the outcome, create the asset, run a test, track the numbers, and then review it properly and intelligently, just like we've discussed.

As you know, only a small proportion of your potential customers are ready to buy now.

That means that some people are thinking about it. A few more are aware that they might need to do something at some point. The biggest single chunk of your market doesn't even know that they need what you have.

You have to be mindful of that.

The small percentage are buying now, but there's the big chunk that isn't actively interested in what you've got RIGHT NOW.

But they will be interested at some point and when you can start to get their attention, if you offer them the right sort of things that are helpful and useful, you can get into their psyche and make sure that when they are ready to buy, they at least think of/ talk to/call or visit you.

It's very, very important this.

Don't be the fool who bemoans the quality of your leads because they're not all 'hot-to-trot' right away. Recognise the game you're playing is a long one.

And that means that you can't do the same old, same old with your marketing.

You can't just do the stuff that everybody else does.

What you want is a *'lead magnet'* for almost every stage.

You have people at different stages of the buying cycle so let's have a lead magnet for all the different stages.

Your lead magnet for those who are ready to buy now might be to book a call or a site visit, or make an appointment.

If you have people who are much further back in the process, your offer to them needs to be much softer. Maybe a 'Buyers Guide', an explainer video or a checklist, say.

You want them to do something – and the easier, more small, the step is that you're asking, the more likely the right people are to take it.

It's a lot easier to do this than most people realise with the right thought.

A lot of the content you need to create really good lead magnets already exist in your business.

It's very rare that you have to go and actually create something completely from scratch.

Then you can have multiple marketing pillars, offering a range of reasons and 'calls-to-action' which will give you a Parthenon-esque marketing system that brings in a consistent, predictable, rhythmic flow of new leads.

CHAPTER TEN:
THE UNDERSTANDING

"Amazing things happen when business owners properly understand their customers..."

Sir Richard Branson

Now whilst it's true that, for all of us, there are lots of people who could buy our stuff, it's much smarter, as a marketer, to focus our marketing efforts on those who should buy our stuff. Our ideal customers.

Your dream buyer is your absolute ideal customer. They're the people who you love to deal with.

They appreciate the work that you do.

They see the world from the same perspective.

Their expectations are realistic.

They're not a pain in the ass.

They pay on time.

They're not price sensitive (and don't quibble over every penny).

They don't give you a hard time.

They're your dream buyer!

When building a dream business, wouldn't it be great to have only your dream customers?

Well then, let's at least start to understand them better so we have a better chance of attracting them.

When it comes to marketing, your audience is everything.

You want to become almost omnipresent to the people who matter to you.

The money and the rhythmic acquisition of customers, in truth, comes from your relationship with your list of potential customers. You can't force a relationship with a list. It's the relationship and the engagement with your list that counts - not the size of your list.

It's much better to have 100 highly engaged prospects on your list than 1,000 who are not engaging with you or paying you any attention. In this regard at least, size doesn't matter!

In our System, we're going to pay attention to not just what we're putting out, but also to how it's consumed.

We send the stuff that gets consumed really well, in other words the emails that get the highest open rates and videos that get the most views, most often.

When you have an asset that resonates, you can send that every three or four months. Because it resonates. Your audience like it. They probably won't remember and even if they do, it doesn't matter because they're at a different time/stage to when they saw it first.

Think about all your marketing collateral as 'assets' to be used repeatedly, as part of a system, to drive the rhythmic acquisition of customers.

Poor results from your marketing almost always come down to not thinking like your customer.

Or from not understanding your customer enough.

You come at things too much from your perspective. Your perspective is about your products, your services and what you do. You know far more about your products and your market than your customers do. You're living and breathing it every day – they're not.

Your ability to see the world through their eyes is in many ways the most important skill of any marketer. To properly think like a customer isn't easy. It takes a lot of conscious effort and many years of practice. Yes, really!

We've all met people and encountered situations where someone is talking about something but they've lost you because they're on a completely different level.
That's what happens in marketing a lot of the time. Insufficient understanding of where the customer is at.

The aim of marketing is to know and understand your customer so well that your product or service just fits them and sells itself.

When you think about it, you'll realise that there's a magical power in feeling understood!

As humans, we are drawn to people who see the world the way we see it. Who think like we think. Who share the same values and priorities as us. That's what 'understanding your ideal customer' is all about.

The Understanding

Getting on their page. Seeing things through their eyes.

Because we understand our customer and since we've written copy that our dream customers are saying yes to; they come to us.

You can write copy like that too.

It's not difficult. It's just words after all. And the right words come easily when you think like your ideal customer.

You just have to understand your customer.

Here's an example from my life:

"For many years I used to drive a Range Rover.

Guy Salmon in Coventry was the dealership that looked after me and they were very good when it came to servicing my car.

I'd like to think this came from a deep understanding of their customer.

What used to happen is they didn't send me postcards in the post saying, *"Your car is due for a service, please give us a ring."*

They understood their customer much better than that.

They used to ring me up and said, *"Mr. Botterill, your Range Rover needs a service. Can I come and collect it a week on Thursday? Does that date work for you? Is your office still up at the business park?"*

"Yes, it is."

"Great! We'll take care of it all."

And they just did it all. They made it really easy for me.

I never quibbled at the price. I never shopped around. I was an ideal customer for them. Because they understood me. I'm busy and they just took care of everything for me."

Not everyone's like that, of course. You might be different. But your ability to understand your ideal customer properly is going to be a decisive factor in your quest to crack the rhythmic acquisition of customers.

There's another lesson from that Range Rover story: save the money on the stamps – just ring people up!

You need to get someone who's sufficiently savvy, switched on and competent to make the calls. You can't hire a brain-dead person. They need to be smart. With personality. And they have to really love talking to people.

Too few business owners recognise the strategic significance of telephone calls.

We're not saying it's a silver bullet, but the proactive use of the telephone can be one of the single best things to move you towards rhythmic acquisition of customers rapidly.
It's getting somebody who's good to ring up the right people on your list, at the right time, just to help them.

Have a conversation. It pulls them closer.

In 99.6% of businesses, more conversations equals more sales.

Another way to crack deep understanding of your customer is to niche down.

When you niche down, you become more relevant to the market, you're niching into which makes it much easier to get people to pay attention and take action.

We helped a garage/MOT centre with their marketing by creating twelve different versions of their A5 flyer that was dropped through letter boxes. The content and message was essentially the same but each version focused on a different car brand. The leaflet put through your door depended on what brand of car was sat on the drive. Niching.

By promoting *'Mercedes specialist servicing'* to Mercedes drivers we got a better response – because the message was more relevant.

Think about it. A leaflet comes through your door offering specialist servicing for the brand of car that you drive. You'll pay more attention to it than you would to a leaflet promoting just independent car servicing.

Niching is powerful because it gives you relevance.

What does a typical day in your dream buyer's life look like? You need to understand that.

Figure out what makes them really happy, not superficially happy.

When you understand that (and it doesn't have to be anything to do with your product or service), you can start to connect with them.

There are ways that you can get in there: phrases, jargon, vernacular.

What's their preferred form of communication?

You have to be very careful here. This is about honing in specifically on the dream customer – not just someone who could be a customer.

Sometimes what's ideal for you may not be ideal for them.

You can't do this thinking superficially.

You have to wonder, why is that? What is it about that?

You have to understand them better than most people do.

What are their biggest frustrations or challenges?

What do they worry about? In the dark of night, if there's something on their minds, what is it?

For example, meeting payroll is something that a lot of business owners worry about because they haven't got sufficient working capital and cash flow in their business. When I talk about *"... pacing the landing in the dark of night wondering how you're going to meet payroll this month"*, my audience relate to that because they've been there and they know that I understand them.

Hopes, dreams, desires – what's it all about for them?

The more you understand your customer, you're giving yourself a better chance of crafting a marketing messages that will resonate with them.

It's not an exercise in itself. It's a means to an end.

Here's a good question for you to think about:

If you only got paid after your customer got the results that you promised, what relevant characteristics would those customers have in order for you to take them on?

So, in order for you to get money, you have to deliver the results that you promised.

What characteristics would your dream client have?

What matching mindsets would you share?

For example, if you ran a high-end bridal store and you were only getting paid after your customer received all the compliments on the big day, what characteristics would your clients need to have?

Obviously, they have to be engaged and get married. You want people for whom this is the most exciting thing ever. So, first-time brides will be better than second-time brides.

Another characteristic will be that they or their family would be *'of means'*, because if you have a bigger budget to play with you can do more amazing stuff.

Then there will almost certainly be a geography. It isn't quite true for every bridal store but if you're going to want people to come and do multiple fittings then enabling you to focus your marketing efforts within 20 – 50 miles of where you are could be a really important thing.

When you go superficially, you're making it harder for yourself to crack rhythmic acquisition.

You're making it more expensive too!

Go deep on the understanding though and you have massive leverage. Huge.

It all comes down to your ability to properly, genuinely and accurately, think like your ideal customer.

CHAPTER ELEVEN:
THE MESSAGE

"I smile whenever I get a message from you..."

In the 1960s, David Ogilvy wrote an article *"How to create advertising that sells"* in which he shares the 38 things that Ogilvy & Mather have learned. A quick Google search will enable you to read it online.

In many ways, Ogilvy really invented modern-day advertising. We've both learned such a lot from studying Ogilvy over the years and this article is a lovely, condensed summary of all the things that help when it comes to creating utterly compelling, differentiating, messages.

The first point that he makes is that the effect of your positioning impacts sales more than anything else.

How do you position your product – or yourself – in your market?

For example, should you position Schweppes as a soft drink or a mixer?

Should you position Dove as a product for dry skin or as a product which gets your hands really clean?

The results of your campaign depend less on how you write your advertising and more on how your product is positioned.

This has implications for all of us as marketers.

The second most important decision, according to Ogilvy, is what you promise the customer?

He explains, *"A promise isn't a claim, or a theme, or slogan. It's a benefit for the consumer. And the product must deliver the benefit you promise."*

When you consider this was written over 60 years ago, the truth of that sentence is still absolutely on the button.

He explains how you should not be a bore, the importance of testimonials and simple headlines, letting your pictures sell the story and avoiding musical backgrounds on TV ads.

In other words, do more of what works!

An utterly compelling differentiating message isn't the same as puking everything about your products all over your customer. It may be memorable, but for different reasons.

When you listen to the radio in the car and you go through a tunnel or into an underground car park, you can lose the signal right? You can't hear anything. It's really frustrating.

We think it's a really good analogy for many businesses.

When the leads aren't coming in and you think your niche is not buying or people won't listen, the reality is that most of the time what's happening is that you're shouting but all your market hears is noise, just like the car radio when you're in the tunnel or the underground car park.

Your message doesn't resonate.

What you've got is dodgy reception.

Sometimes to cut through the dodgy reception and get your message heard, it takes less rather than more.

Simplicity can be very powerful.

When you're writing your marketing, develop your messages with the clear understanding that your recipient will be stubbornly reluctant to both receive your message and believe your message.

It's very rare that someone wakes up in the morning hoping that you're going to market to them.

That doesn't happen.

You have to fight for their attention in what's already a very busy day.

They're thinking about themselves, their kids, their spouse, their money, their health, their next holiday, the new car they're hoping to get, their pet, their hobbies, their golf day, their new clothes, their parking ticket, their hair appointment, their repeat prescription, happy hour *(!)*, the football this weekend, filling up with petrol, their dry cleaning, picking up some milk on the way home, what's for dinner tonight, the new boxset on Netflix, the weather this weekend, replacing the bulb in the bathroom and then, and only then... your marketing!

You need to recognise that they'll be stubbornly reluctant to receive your marketing.

They'll be stubbornly reluctant to read or watch your marketing.

And they'll be stubbornly reluctant to believe your message.

So, your marketing has to work really hard to get their attention.

And the fact is, most marketing doesn't work hard at all. It makes a cursory attempt to get the reader's attention. As a consequence, it makes it really easy for your prospects to ignore you completely and put your collateral straight in the (real or virtual) bin.

But once somebody has responded, you can begin to nurture that relationship.

Here at EC, we're in a very fortunate position. We have tens of thousands of people who read our messages with a degree of enthusiasm, but that's because we've been nurturing them for quite a long time.

It wasn't like that in the beginning. We had to work really hard to overcome that stubbornness, as we all do when it comes to penetrating our markets.

We've found that three things have really helped us when it comes to building an audience and getting our marketing messages 'consumed':

Firstly, **don't be boring.**

You shouldn't be boring, because most people in your market are boring.

This was true in the 1960s *(as you heard from David Ogilvy)* and it's definitely true now.

The second thing is **just try and help people**. Commercially what we've learned is that it's a really smart thing to do. When you're generous with your knowledge and expertise and you genuinely help people they warm to you, they pay attention and their propensity to buy from you *(at some point)* goes up massively.

Show them that you can help them by actually helping them. Quite a trick eh!

And what we've discovered is that the more you help people, the faster the business grows.

Which really feeds into rule number three:

Make it all about them!

Not 90% about them and a little bit about you.

Not 99% about them and 1% about you.

Make it ALL about them.

Just focus on them, their situation, their problem, their choice, or their desires.

Make it all about them!

When it comes to crafting your message, with this approach,

you'll definitely have more success.

So what has to happen when you're crafting your message?

Well, first up, the 'temperature' of your marketing must match the temperature of your audience or your traffic.

You have audiences at different temperatures.

You have people who are 'hot-to-trot'. They're ready to buy. Good marketing messages for people who are 'hot-to-trot' are *"call for a quote"* or *"fill in this form to arrange a meeting"*, or even *"buy now"*.

Unfortunately many websites and marketing pieces only have *'hot-to-trot'* messages – which are too hot for most of their visitors.

If I'm lukewarm, or just investigating whether to buy, the message that I need from you needs to be a much cooler message.

It shouldn't be about buy now.

For example, one message from an EC member that we saw recently on LinkedIn read: *"If you know that you ought to be doing more on LinkedIn to get leads and sales for your business, but you're not sure what to do about it, here's a free guide that will tell you everything you need to know."*

That's a very compelling offer.

And when we spoke with that guy what we found is that he's shipping hundreds of those guides a week!

And the content he's giving them is really good.

People get the guide - it's 36 pages and super-helpful - and what happens is that people try to do it themselves but, over a three month window, and thanks to consistent, systematic, rhythmic follow-up from him, about one in twelve of those who get the guide ask him to do some work for them to help them with lead generation through LinkedIn.

Really smart strategy.

If he went out there saying *"Buy LinkedIn Service now,"* he'd get some sales, but he'd miss a big chunk of the market.

His lead generation message is at the right *'temperature'* for his market.

This means that when you're starting to craft your utterly compelling messages, you need multiple ones (at least two or three) to account for the different temperatures of the different parts of your market.

Now, other things that you've got to crack when it comes to putting your message together is WHY should they choose you?

Why should your potential customers dip into their hard-earned cash and spend some of it with you as opposed to all of the other choices that they have?

To rise up the pyramid you have to have a good answer to that.

Your message can't just be: *"We do X"* or *"We do X and we do it really well..."*

You somehow have to emerge and stand out.

Ogilvy's number one thing was positioning. How do you position this product or business?

How do you want to be seen and perceived in the marketplace?

Just imagine for a moment that in the room next door to wherever you're sat right now, there are 500 of your ideal dream customers.

They're all waiting to hear from you.

In a moment, I'm going to go next door and introduce you to them.

When I stand up on stage to introduce you, what do you want me to say?

How should I introduce you to 500 of your dream customers?

That's how you get the answer to this question!

That introduction starts to position you in the right way for your ideal market.

And once you've crafted it, that message starts to appear in all your marketing; it's your positioning.

Why should they choose you?

If you think of this marketing system as a piece of machinery *(which of course it's not because it needs quite a bit of creative human input)* then getting the message wrong is like sticking a big crowbar into the cogs.

It will stop the system.

If your message isn't right, everything else will cease to function.

You have to get the message right.

Getting your message right can be the difference between languishing in mediocrity in the middle of the pyramid and soaring to the top.

You have to get comfortable with what you are from the perspective of your customer. To do this properly you have to be sufficiently bold and interesting. And definitely not boring.

If you can craft into your messaging a really clear reason why your ideal customer should at least talk to you, you have a decent chance.

We know how hard this can be. And how uncomfortable it makes a lot of people.

You sometimes will need help to do this well.

You're articulating what you are and why they should choose you.

You're not creating fairy tales. It has to be absolutely grounded in truth. But it also needs to be self-aggrandizing.

It all starts with properly understanding your ideal customer.

CHAPTER TWELVE:
THE R.U.C

"Just be useful.

Always be helping..."

R.U.C is just Really Useful Content. That's all.

Honestly, it's so much easier to produce Really Useful Content than most people realise.

In your mind it becomes a big, challenging job. It's not your natural space. How am I going to write this? How I'm going to create this?

Well, the good news is, it's a lot simpler than most people realise.

First of all, it doesn't have to be 27 pages long. Sometimes, a single sheet can be really good.

It doesn't have to take you a long time to create either, because you know a lot of stuff.

When you follow the guidance of Marcus Sheridan from his book 'They Ask You Answer' and create your Knowledge Centre on your website, you're well on the way to creating a ton of R.U.C.

You know your stuff.

You've just got to get it out.

You've done the hard yards over the last 10 – 20 years.

You know your market. You know the problems that your ideal customers are facing because you happily, willingly, and eagerly talk about all those things to your customers, staff and prospects on a daily basis.

All you have to do to produce Really Useful Content is just start to capture what you're doing anyway.

The best way we've found to do that is by just talking.

We use the Rev app on our phones. *(Rev.com)*.

All you do is turn Rev on, talk to yourself and hit submit when you're finished.

Usually within the hour, a beautifully typed Word document appears in your inbox, courtesy of the clever people at Rev.

What you've got then is a good first draft, but it will usually need a bit of further work just to *'polish'* it.

That's how we write everything.

You might have written articles in the past. You've written stuff for your brochure and website. You have a lot of stuff that's locked in your cupboard. It went out once as an email in 2012, but it's still valid today.

Get it out. Dust it off. Update it.

It's not difficult to create R.U.C. Just follow these three rules:

R.U.C RULE 1
Attention-grabbing headlines and titles
You have to get into the mind of your ideal customer.

What's going to appeal to them?

Your headline/title exists solely to 'sell' your R.U.C to your ideal customer. It's not there to summarise what the content is all about.

R.U.C RULE 2
Make sure that every point touches a burning issue.

What you don't want to do is produce lots of bland, banal, beige content that no one cares about.

You can't state the bleedin' obvious.

Make it useful and address a burning issue. Which means it has to be useful and informative to your reader.

People just want the insight.

They want the little nugget.

They want the stuff that's useful. That's a R.U.C.

When your content touches on genuinely burning issues, you'll be amazed at the response.

One IFA in EC wrote a 400 word article (using Rev!) back in 2016 about dividend payments and pension contributions for business owners. That one little article still brings her leads every single month almost five years on – because it is super-specific and addresses a genuine burning issues if you're a business owner with that particular problem. It's a great example of a R.U.C.

Once you have a collection of R.U.Cs, it's so much easier to systemise the dissemination of your content – and it can become systemised and repeatable - because you have the content.

Without R.U.Cs, your system is impotent. Unable to function.

It's a lot easier to sell or market a guide on the seven mistakes to avoid when hiring a financial planner than it is to sell a meeting with a financial planner.

But once you have someone who's downloaded that guide, you have a prospect.

Then, you can start to nurture your relationship with him/her. You can offer help and, at the right time, suggest a phone call or a meeting. When you provide the right R.U.C, you'll find that some of your prospects actually contact you asking for a call or meeting. Boom!

But when you try and go for the kill at the beginning – and in this instance, that would mean your marketing is selling the call or meeting - you'll fail because they don't know and trust you enough.

There's no relationship at this point.

And the money - and rhythmic acquisition - are in the relationship.

To build the relationship, you have to give of yourself.

That's what this is about. It's not some new theory. It's predicated on an understanding of human behaviour through the ages.

Ignore it and you're condemning yourself to a life in the bottom half of the pyramid.

RUC RULE 3
Don't make your R.U.C complicated.

Our third little rule is the bit that gets you out of jail.

This is the bit that stops R.U.Cs from being a big deal *(for you to produce)* because you can't make your R.U.C complicated.

And you can't make it big and long.

You're not writing a 10,000-word book because you don't need one.

I mean, when did you last download a 44-page eBook AND actually read it?

Doesn't happen often, right?

So why would you expect someone to do the same with yours? Don't confuse size with quality.

Don't think that you have to do something big for it to be worthwhile.

You simply have to match the temperature of your audience. Where are people at?

We have a range of different types of RUCs. The following are some examples that you could use.

1. Checklists and Cheat Sheets
(A Cheat Sheet is typically a single sheet of paper that tells people what to do).

2. Quizzes
These can be good for certain markets and audiences. Test their knowledge. It can work very well.

3. Video
We find videos super-effective. In most markets people are really comfortable watching videos online and they're really easy to do now.

There's still a great reluctance to do them though, especially amongst business owners. People get stuck in a 'I'm-not-worthy-enough' state. But you are worthy!

You know your stuff and you're passionate about it. And that's what people will buy.

The world is full of people who are good on video now, but they weren't born that way. They just started doing it. Which is what you should do.

4. Toolkits *(can be good.)*
We had a great R.U.C that worked well for several years that provided people with a set of templates to write a particular piece of marketing. It was a toolkit.

5. Live Demos
They may morph into different things. Sometimes you

might do a live demo onto a piece of video that goes out as a video.

6. Email Courses

An email course sounds a lot grander than it is. Typically it would be a series of 7 – 8 emails sent over 8 – 10 days. It just breaks something up into 7 – 8 chunks, each of which is about a page in length. That's all. It's a lovely repurposed thing. That can be a brilliant generator of high quality leads in lots of markets.

7. Physical product

We have a *'swipe file'* of great marketing collateral that works very well to get prospects engaged with us. We offer it as a download.

8. Infographics

These are great in certain markets, and again it's not difficult to do an infographic. Just simplify something for people *(which infographics are great at)* and you can be on a home-run in terms of relationships and getting them to talk with you.

[By the way, the best way to get an infographic produced is to use Upwork.com. You sketch it out on a piece/pieces of paper and then use Upwork to find a designer who can turn your scribbles into a beautiful infographic. It will normally cost $50 - $100 and be done in 48 hours!]

9. White Paper

Be careful with these but in some instances when you have a lot of stuff to talk about, white papers can be a nice way to present it. A white paper makes it feel a lot more official. It shows your knowledge. It won't apply in every market, but will apply to some.

10. eBooks and Real Books
Real books are better than eBooks. Real books are much easier to produce than most people realise and their impact is usually much greater.

11. Webinars and Online Training
They need a bit of preparation, but not a lot in most cases because you're talking about the stuff that you know all about.

If you choose smartly, these assets will serve you for years in most cases. Not just for months.

You now have pillars all over the place that are starting to bring people into your funnel.

Once they're in your funnel, you can nurture them, help them and keep in contact with them.

And every time you do that, your reputation is enhanced.

Things start to grow. All of a sudden, you have a business that's a million miles away from where it started out. You have an audience that's paying attention to you, that's talking to you, that's buying from you. And before you know it, you realise that you've moved markedly up the pyramid.

That's why R.U.C matters.

Businesses that only ever shout *"buy me now!"* never get near the top of the pyramid. Because you can't build a business by just aiming at the 3% of the marketplace.

CHAPTER THIRTEEN:
THE DON...

"I'm gonna make him an offer he can't refuse"

Vito Corleone (from Mario Puzo's The Godfather)

I love watching The Godfather films.

Although they're almost fifty years old, they're still absolute cinematic classics with a great story to boot.

Of course, the most famous line is when Marlon Brando as Don Vito Corleone says, *"I'm gonna make him an offer that he can't refuse..."*

Obviously, it's said in a very frightening way in the movie, but from a marketing perspective it can be a hugely useful benchmark for us to use.

You see, a lot of marketing fails because of weak, insipid offers. Offers that were really easy to ignore or refuse.

There are fundamentally two parts to any offer:

1. What your prospect's going to get when they respond to your marketing?

2. What they have to do to get it?

Some people screw up the second bit by making it too difficult or hard for people to get it.

But many more mess up the first bit because the biggest problem is that they have very resistible offers.

They're a country mile away from an offer that people can't refuse.

Don Corleone would be ashamed of the offers made by many businesses today.

So, the trick to creating a Don Corleone offer is to offer something that people want. In that regard, your R.U.C can become a Don Corleone offer, because all it takes is a click and all of a sudden, your pool of leads flowing in is now much higher.

You have to build the value up until it becomes irresistible. It can be a helpful exercise to go through what would have to happen for you to make your offer so attractive that it would be literally impossible for your ideal customer to NOT take it up.

Come on, think about it...

...if your life depended on your ideal customer seeing your marketing and then taking you up on whatever you were offering, what would your offer be?

Does what you're currently offering even come close?

We're not saying this is easy – but in our experience few things worth having in life are.

And the prize when you get it right can be life-changing. The systematic, rhythmic acquisition of customers.

Value can be found in different places when it's sold properly.

A lot of times, a bigger problem for businesses is actually that you hide away the stuff that you do anyway.

Here's an example of how a cleaning company has used a strong guarantee to create an offer that the Don would be proud of:

Stewart's cleaning company specialises in cleaning pubs and clubs in the night-time leisure industry. One of the worst things, if you run a pub or a club, is to turn up for work at 10:30am and find your cleaner hasn't been in. When this happens, you have a big problem.

That's the first big problem the market has. Unreliability.

So, we created a compelling Don Corleone offer by providing a unique 'you'll-never-miss-a-clean-ever' guarantee. If you do, Stewart's company will pay you £1,000.

This message is genuinely very compelling because everyone running a pub has, at some point in the past, come into work and found their cleaner hasn't turned up.

Now Stewart's company wasn't missing cleans. In fact, he hasn't missed a clean in three years, because he has a unique system to ensure that it can never happen.

So, we turned what he was doing anyway into a really strong guarantee – and explained the system behind it to give his new prospects real confidence.

All we did here was dress up what Stewart was already doing, but we presented it in a different way.

This is a living, breathing manifestation of creating an utterly compelling differentiating message.

But Stewart didn't stop there.

He knew his market had two other very real problems that he could fix. One concerned the quality of the clean and auditing and the other was around supplies of cleaning product for the cleaners. He dealt with both of them in an utterly compelling way – again offering 'no-questions-asked' £1,000 guarantees if the company failed to deliver.

There's probably something that you do already in your business that can be turned into a compelling offer and guarantee in the way that Stewart did. All you have to do is flick the switch that allows you to think in a slightly different way about what you're already doing so that you can present it in a genuinely, utterly compelling manner to your target market...

What you're up against is that you're so deep into your business that you can't see the wood for the trees. You can't see the differentiating factors that already exist.

Promising quality and great customer service isn't enough. It just washes over people. I'm not saying that they're unimportant, but they're not irresistible – and often not believable - when it comes to creating offers.

You have to take responsibility as the marketer of your business to create offers that zing *(and actually work)*.

With a lot of marketing, the problem often comes down to your offer because what you're offering just isn't sufficiently exciting or compelling enough for your customers to want it.

If your marketing is just saying *"this is what we do..."* you will get some customers.

Like when Stewart's marketing said that "we specialise in cleaning pubs and clubs", he did get some new customers. But it wasn't enough to move him up the pyramid.

If you ever find yourself complaining - even just to yourself - that not enough people are buying from you, recognise firstly that it's your fault; and secondly that the solution can often be to make your offer more irresistible.

Do a bit extra.

Add more value.

Make it more convenient.

Make it faster, cheaper or better.

Use scarcity.

Nine times out of 10, if you're not selling as much as you want or you're not getting the response that you want, it comes down to the offer.

You're in full control of this.

You get to choose what you offer to the market.

And when you understand your numbers and the value of a new customer it's often by changing the offer, or creating the offer differently, that you can dramatically change the results you get – just like Stewart did.

Random Doors

Imagine walking up to a door, knowing that what's behind the door is good. Very good. Life changingly good.

You then pick one random key to try to open the door, but it doesn't fit the lock.

You feel sad. You give up and you never try again.

That is how most people approach marketing.

Bonkers isn't it.

Why would you walk away from a door behind which there are so many riches for you? Especially after only one (or possibly two!) tries. Yet that's what most business owners do.

There's a much better way to crack the door.

A scientific, systematic way.

First, you make sure you're trying to get through the right door. That's the niche and their problem. That's what you're going after.

Next, you do the research to make sure that the people behind the door want what you've got. Do people really need what you're selling?

This research helps make sure that you have the best possible guess at the key that will open it because you then create a niche offer that you think will open the door.

You have the niche. That's who you're going after. That's your desired result.

The bit you can play around with is the offer.

What can you do to make your service or products appropriately attractive to your niche to get you through the door? You have to create a sufficiently compelling offer in all its guises. One that's not about money off or slashing your prices.

Now, your first offer (the key!) probably won't work. If it does you're very, very, very lucky.

In all our experience, it's very rare that you come up with a killer offer at the first attempt.

So, you test it. You try different things.

You think this will open the door, and you then try it and see.

What do your numbers say?

The numbers are how the System works. Marketing is creativity plus maths, remember.

So, you test it. You look at the numbers. You test it again. And again if necessary.

That's how you get to a place where you have a killer offer.

You systemise the testing until you get an offer that works. A key that unlocks the door.

CHAPTER FOURTEEN:
THE MEDIA

"Whoever controls the media, controls the mind"

Jim Morrison

Media is just a way to get your *(utterly compelling, differentiating)* message to your market.

That's all it is.

You're going to ask yourself the very sensible question: *"What is the best media to get my message to my market?"*

The best answers to that question come from your deep understanding of your customers.

You're going to pick multiple media, do them properly (one or two at a time so you don't get overwhelmed) and then track the results.

Some media will be a much more obvious fit than others – but please don't dismiss any without careful thought.

The best way to 'test' different media is to use an existing offer *(and creative)* that you know works. That way you're only testing one variable.

If you try a new offer in a new media and it doesn't work, you'll never know whether it was the offer or the media that didn't work.

When you have something that works as an offer, you can roll that through different media.

So, by far the best way to find out if a media will work for you is to go to that media with a piece of creative and an offer that has already worked somewhere else.

You know that the message/offer combo works and so what you're now testing is the media.

If you go to a new media with an established message and offer that has worked, you massively reduce the chances of making a bad decision.

You'll test it. You'll iterate. You'll test again, until it works. Then, you'll take those messages and offers and roll them through other marketing pillars. There's no more complexity to this part of the system than that.

The complexity comes in getting the messages and offers right.

Then, the fun starts.

Nurturing

When you want to build a long-term relationship with potential customers, that relationship needs nurturing. That means you have to put effort in. You have to follow-up.

For almost every business, the quickest and easiest way to increase sales and, therefore, get closer to the rhythmic acquisition of customers, is to get better at handling and managing the leads that you're already getting or already have.

That will normally be the quickest and best way by far to accelerate your revenue and profitability.

It will also be a lot, lot easier *(and way cheaper!)* than getting loads more leads.

Why would you want to focus on putting even more leads in and spending more money to get more leads when you're putting them into a system which currently isn't anywhere close to optimum?

The truth is no one is doing the follow-up as well as they can.

It's always possible to enhance the quality and in most cases, the quantity of your follow-up.

People need to be reminded of you in the right way, on a lot of occasions, before they'll buy from you.

You may have seen the following truism before. It ostensibly dates back to Victorian times but it is absolutely applicable nowadays:

How Many Times Should You Advertise?

The first time, they don't even see your ad.

The second time, they don't notice it.

The third time, they glance at it.

The fourth time, they got a fleeting sense that they've seen it before.

The fifth time, they actually read the ad.

The sixth time, they thumb their nose at it.

The seventh time, they're getting irritated.

The eighth time, there's that ad again.

The ninth time, they start to wonder if they're missing out on something.

The tenth time, they ask their friend if he has tried it.

The eleventh time, they wonder how the company's paying for all these ads.

The twelfth time, they start to think it must be a good product.

The thirteenth time, they start to see the product's value.

The fourteenth time, they remember wanting a product like this for a long time.

The fifteenth time, they start to yearn for it, but can't afford to buy it.

The sixteenth time, they accept that they will buy it sometime in the future.

The seventeenth time, they make a note to buy it.

The eighteenth time, they curse their poverty for not allowing them to buy this terrific product.

The nineteenth time, they count their money very carefully.

The twentieth time, they buy what's offered.

As we've said before, if you think you can build the systematic rhythmic acquisition of customers by just going after the 3% who are ready to buy now, you genuinely are bonkers.

Most businesses don't follow up more than once or twice at most.

At four contacts, almost 90% have given up.

By five follow-up attempts, 95% of businesses have given up.

But on the fifth follow-up, you're now becoming a factor in the prospect's mind.

Contact six and seven, the prospect now starts to know who you are.

By contact eight or nine, if you're doing it properly, you're starting to earn top-of-mind awareness.

At contact 10, you're probably the only one left standing.

No one has ever contacted them 10 times. Once you get here, it means that when they're ready to buy, you've got a 90% chance of at least getting a shot at it. They'll at least talk to you. It doesn't guarantee you'll get the deal or business, but it does mean you'll get considered if you're keeping in touch and nurturing that relationship in the right way.

Simple things done well look good. Especially when it comes to follow up!

You don't have to complicate it. There's really no need.

You don't have to create wonderfully complex newsletters and send them out in the post. Just keep in touch in the right kind of way.

So what's the right kind of way?

Well, we're glad you asked*(!)*

Here's what a world class follow up system looks like:

- A new lead comes in.

- You call that lead within 10 minutes of the lead coming in. If there's an answer, you have a conversation. *(They'll be stunned that you've called 'em so quick and that first impression will go a long way to help you build your relationship).*

  On the conversation, you listen carefully and understand a bit more about what they're looking for. In some cases, there'll be enough information gathered and an appointment will be booked.

- If there's no answer, you try again *(four attempts at a call within the first couple of hours).*

- If you leave it more than four hours before you call people, you're really out of the game.

  Because the world we live in today is a busy one. Everyone's busy. If we don't get a reply, we move on.

The Entrepreneurs Marketing System

A World Class Follow Up System...

Following up an enquiry within 10 minutes is four times more likely to result in a sale than if you wait longer than four hours. If this is a new lead enquiring about your business and you leave it four hours (which doesn't seem like that long), what the statistics reveal is that people have moved on. It's so easy now for people to find someone else to ring because there's that thing called Google.

When the prize that you're chasing is that ideal life for yourself and the people you love, you recognise that you have to get this in place to work. Screwing this up is what kills you, because these are on a plate.

- If after trying three or four times to talk to them on the telephone and you still didn't get an answer, a text message is sent just to let people know that you've received their enquiry and if you can help they should give you a ring.

- If they text back a reply, that will normally lead to a conversation.

- Using the BombBomb video messaging app as part of your follow-up is a great way to accelerate yourself up that relationship ladder with your prospects.

People are more likely to want to remain in contact and spend money with you when they know you better and BombBomb is a brilliant tool for doing that. It comes with a fantastic tracking system as well so you know when people have opened your email and when they've watched your video.

BombBomb is also really quick and easy to do. It's way quicker to send someone a BombBomb than it is to write them a message.

- Once you've spoken with your prospect and arranged an appointment or scheduled a call, there's the confirmation email to send.

- Then, there's a reminder email a couple of days before the appointment and a reminder text on the day of the appointment.

That may look like quite a lot, or feel really complicated, but actually when you break it down it isn't either.

What we've just described is the first phase follow up system of a professional business person who is on his or her way to the top of the pyramid.

Recognise that if/when you start to compromise on this system and you think, for instance, *"I don't need to call 'em within 10 minutes"* that you are holding yourself back down the pyramid.

Recognise that the price you're paying for not using BombBomb is you're moving further and further away from that defined life that you mapped out.

Now, Phase One follow up relates to handling those initial enquiries but how do you keep in touch on an ongoing basis?

That's where Phase Two comes in...

You don't want your prospects to feel stalked or pestered or spammed.

You want them to feel cared for. But almost everybody screws this up. They either do too much or too little.

The truth is that there are many more businesses right now that are screwing up the follow-up by doing too little than by doing too much.

Statistically, you're almost certainly in the 'not-doing-enough' camp. It's quite difficult to get from the 'not-doing-enough' camp to the 'doing-too-much' camp.

Look, acquiring new customers is the most expensive thing in almost any business. It's also one of the most difficult. Therefore, why would you give up so early? Why would you stop with your follow-up?

There's no logical reason why you would stop.

And if you start by doing just a little bit more follow-up than you are at present, you'll start to see the results coming through.

Rhythmic acquisition is always preceded by rhythmic activity, remember.

And the most important piece of rhythmic activity is the deployment of proper follow-up throughout your business.

A really great way to get your follow-up back on track if it's been a bit neglected is the three-line email.

It's so effective and simple. It's really informal and personalised. It can be used by anyone!

You can pick your subject line. Just a quickie like:
"Mike, can I help?"

Then, there are the three lines.

> *"Hi Mike,*
>
> *Just wondering if you're still looking for (whatever it is that you do)?*
>
> *If so, I'd love to help..."*

Any corporate speak from that email has been obliterated so that it feels personal.
You can screw up the three-line email when you write it like a corporate dork as it will feel like it's being sent to everybody.

Send this email out to your list and you'll get conversions.
It will build relationships.

You'll get people coming back to you and telling you about things that are happening.

And your follow-up is off and running again...

Phase Two follow up is when you send out your articles, your newsletters, your birthday cards, etc.

The Media

One size does not fit all. Your messages shouldn't be the same to everybody. Whenever your list naturally segments, so should your messaging.

If you persist in treating all customers and prospects the same with your messaging, by definition what you do is you start to lose people. The relationship wanes. They think that you care less and that you understand them less.

The more personal and bespoke each piece of follow up FEELS, the more successful it will become. And they mustn't all be selling.

The System recognises that actually when you're using media and you're going out proactively with your follow-up to nurture your list, you need to be prepared to segment.

You use the simple tools that make that segmentation straightforward and easy.

It's getting harder and harder to get penetration/readership on email for instance, but it gets easier to get open rates up on email when you have a relationship.

When your emails that you send stack up well on the collateral quality test (in other words they're useful and not boring), you can still get very good open rates.

Broadly speaking, the more emails you send, the more money you'll make. And vice versa.

The more money you make, the closer you get to the ideal life that you defined.

223

What happens, though, is that people stress too much about unsubscribes. They worry about the tiny number of people who might complain about receiving their emails.

Remember, the big gorilla marketers? Their numbers don't care about your feelings!

The only thing that really matters is the numbers.

If you're not getting unsubscribes, you're in a lot of trouble because you're definitely not sending enough stuff out.

People stress too much about unsubscribes. Numbers trump feelings.

The people who matter won't mind. And those who mind really don't matter because they weren't ever going to buy.

That's worth repeating: **the people who unsubscribe were never going to buy.**

Your list is better without them. Don't worry about it.
See it as a positive. It means you're doing your job properly.

Broadly speaking, when it comes to your follow-up, you're pursuing the dream life that you mapped out and designed. That means that you have to be prepared to 'put it out there'.

Do the follow-up! Just make contact. Get in touch.
Help them – and occasionally ask 'em to buy.

As well as regular emails, the odd item in the post, maybe an occasional text message or phone call.

Pop Quiz:

Q: What's costing you tens of thousands of pounds in lost sales?

A: Getting leads with phone numbers and NOT ringing them up.

These are leads that have given you their phone number.

You had the sense to ask for it on your lead form.

You haven't made it compulsory, but they put a phone number on there.

What logical reason would you have for not trying to ring those people?

These are not cold calls. They've given you their number. The sooner you call them, the more obvious, logical and less 'salesy' it is.

Make friends and help 'em.

That's all you're doing.

You'll be stunned at what happens when you do this.

And life becomes more fun because you're making a lot of friends, helping a lot of people and pulling them closer to you. With follow-up.

Your job at this point is to start thinking and look at what follow-up will work.

Do the things that will make the biggest impact first.

Keep in touch with them until they buy or until they die *(or say "stop sending me stuff!").*

Until they say that, we send stuff that will inform, educate, and help them.

We'll try to make 'em smile occasionally, because that helps build relationships. Plus, more people will buy.

Your system needs this genuinely high-quality nurturing of your list.

Without it, you will fall short of where you want to be.
With it, when it's done properly, you have the potential to drive up your sales exponentially and, at the same time, ascend the pyramid.

What you're doing is harvesting a bigger chunk of the market and nurturing them.

You're building a relationship with them.

You're helping them.

You're building your reputation.

That's what your follow up is all about.

CHAPTER FIFTEEN:
THE SCORE

*"If you can't read the scoreboard
you don't know the score. If you
don't know the score you can't tell
the winners from the losers"*

Warren Buffett

You have to know the score.

In February 2017, Paris St Germain thumped the mighty Barcelona 4-0 in a Champions League Round-of-16 match in Paris.

Three weeks later, at the Nou Camp, 96,290 Barcelona fans turned out to support their side in the second leg despite the heavy defeat they'd suffered in the first game.

Barcelona's Luis Suárez scored the first goal of the game in the 3rd minute and just before half-time, an own goal made it 2-0 to Barca.

Lionel Messi converted a penalty on 50 minutes to make it 3-0 but Barcelona's hopes of an extraordinary comeback were crushed when Edinson Cavani scored for PSG in the 62nd minute, leaving them requiring three more to win due to the away goals rule.

Neymar scored two goals in the closing stages – a free kick in the 88th minute and a penalty kick in the 91st – to make it 5–1.

It still wasn't enough, until, in the final seconds of the match, a speculative cross into the PSG penalty area was met by Sergi Roberto, who scored Barcelona's sixth and final goal in the 95th minute, thus winning the game 6–1 and advancing to the quarter finals 6–5 on aggregate.

The media went wild and the game was widely acclaimed as having been the best comeback ever.

But here's the thing: it wouldn't have happened if the Barcelona team hadn't known the score.

Think about it. They knew they were in a hole. They knew at the start that they had to score five times to win, and then, when PSG scored they had to get six to prevail.

There is no way they would have pushed so hard to score three goals after the 88th minute if they hadn't known the score and what they had to do.

That's the power of the scoreboard.

Warren Buffett said,

> *"If you can't read the scoreboard, you don't know the score. And if you don't know the score, you can't tell the winners from the losers."*

Buffett is right.

Barcelona were right.

To win at business, to climb to the heady heights atop the pyramid, you have to know the score.

So, how do you tell the winners from the losers?

The 12 Key Numbers are the absolute core running through this system.

You have to understand and know these numbers.

They're what tell you the absolute score in your business.

The Entrepreneurs Marketing System

How do you keep track of the different marketing pieces? Tracking it per month can be a good place to start.

The easiest way is to create a spreadsheet like the one shown opposite.

Down the left-hand column, you have all your marketing pillars. Across the top, you have the days of the week (you would typically include the weekends here). All you're doing at this point is you're tracking the leads that are coming in and where they're coming in from.

Now it gets a little bit more complicated.

In the second half of this spreadsheet, you start to look at what happens to these leads. So, for example, you might track the meetings that you've booked.

Then, you can also track your proposals that were sent.

You also track the sales value. Similarly, you can do your average sales amount.

You then get your meeting conversion rates and proposal conversion rates.

The other things you can track are the unsubscribes on email. If you get three zero days in a row, you're not doing enough. You want unsubscribes from your emails, because that shows that you have emails and stuff going out.

*(You can download the spreadsheet opposite and all the other tools referenced in this book at **EMSSystem.co.uk/downloads**)*

Marketing Tracker

Date		TOTAL	Day/Date
Google Ads		62	Google Ads
Organic web traffic		1	Organic web traffic
Walk-in's		1	Walk-in's
Referrals		2	Referrals
Facebook Ad's		28	Facebook Ad's
LinkedIn		1	LinkedIn
YouTube		1	YouTube
Instagram		6	Instagram
Leaflet Drop		23	Leaflet Drop
Magazine		3	Magazine
		0	
Total		128	
Running Total			
Average Daily Leads		4.6	
Meetings Booked		21	Meetings Booked
Proposal Sent		18	Proposal Sent
New Clients		15	New Clients
Sales Value			Sales Value
Average Sale Amount			Average Sale Amount
Meeting Conversion Rate			Meeting Conversion Rate
Proposal Conversion Rate			Proposal Conversion Rate
Unsubscribes from Email			Unsubscribes from Email
Total Unique Visits to Website			Total Unique Visits to Website
No. of people enrolled			No. of people enrolled

Cost per Lead & Cost per Sale

	Spent	Leads	Cost/Lead	Sales	Cost/Sale
Google Ads	£345	62	£6		
Organic web traffic	£1	1	£1		
Walk-in's	£1	1	£1		
Referrals	£1	2	£1		
Facebook Ad's	£292	28	£10		
LinkedIn	£1	1	£1		
YouTube	£1	1	£1		
Instagram	£56	6	£9		
Leaflet Drop	£345	23	£15		
Magazine	£99	3	£33		
	£1,837	128	£12		£101

You can also track the unique visits to your website.

Collating this information isn't difficult. You could easily delegate it to a PA. But having it captured each day makes a massive difference – because now you know the score.

Congratulations. You're now professional business person.

Only when you start to track it and see it visibly every day do the numbers start to become real and mean something.

Like anything else, when you start to care about it and see it, it gets more attention. That attention then helps to build momentum and before you know it you're moving meaningfully towards your defined life. You're Barcelona. You know the score.

The power of this tracker can't be underestimated.

What have you spent on marketing so far this month?

How many leads did you get?

Your cost per lead is then a straightforward sum.

How many sales have come through a specific marketing pillar, such as Google Ads?

What's your cost per sale?

Where are you not spending money?

Now you start to see where it all works. You can start to see the dials and where you should be putting your energy, your effort, and your money becomes really clear.

To be clear, make your scoreboard your own. Personalise and tailor it for your business. Track the things that matter for you.

The fundamentals are all there. It's just an Excel spreadsheet. But it tells you whether your system is working and getting better or if your system isn't working or getting worse.

The really smart thing to do is to make other people responsible for populating this spreadsheet.

Your job is to evaluate it, review it, and understand what's happening.

When you start to get this in place, you start to see what's happening. It's the business equivalent of bringing sight to the blind. And when you can see what's happening, and where you're going, your chances of moving markedly up the pyramid increase dramatically.

This Marketing Tracker is what ensures that you're driving rhythmic activity.

And if you haven't got rhythmic activity, you don't get the rhythmic acquisition of customers. Ever.

But when you start getting rhythmic lead flow every single day then your rhythmic acquisition will start to come through.

This Marketing Tracker is just such a helpful, useful tool for every business.

It brings everything together.

But it's only part of keeping score.

The second part is your Scorecard.

Your Scorecard goes beyond just your marketing.

When thinking about your Scorecard, imagine that you're stranded on a desert island.

The good news is that you're not going to starve. You have access to food and water, BUT you aren't contactable by your business.

No phone, no internet. Nothing. You're cut off.

But what arrives every week is a single piece of paper and on it will be a handful of numbers that must allow you to have an absolute pulse on your business.

So, what would your handful of numbers be?

What would you need to know that would tell you, instantly, whether things were good, bad, on track or off track in your business?

Going back to our optician example that we looked at earlier, the two key numbers would be:

- Number of eye tests this week

- Average transaction value.

  The Scorecard might also include:

- Total Revenue this week

When you think about it, because the costs of running the practice are so fixed, these three numbers would give you a 99% accurate picture as to how that business was doing.

And when you track the numbers weekly and have a rolling 13 week set of numbers on your single sheet of paper, you can see the trends and direction as well as the actual figures. Well welcome to the Professional Business Persons Club. You're now an honorary life member.

With your Marketing Tracker and your Business Scorecard in place, you have eyes on the right numbers to drive your business to where you want it to be and to move yourself way, way up the pyramid.

A couple of insights when it comes to working out your Scorecard numbers:

Firstly, weekly numbers are best.

Activity-based numbers are key – i.e. numbers that people in the business can do something about.

Track 'inputs' not just 'outputs'.

So, taking an optician, for instance, an 'input' number could be how many eye tests are booked over the next two weeks *(so you have an early indication as to what's going to happen in the future to 'Eye Tests This Week')* as opposed to *'Eye Tests This Week'* which is a definite 'output' number.

If you do track the right numbers here, you should be able to see any problems before they happen because you'll be tracking the alerts.

So, for instance, if you received no leads this week then there'll be a week in the future when you'll make no sales.

Now, if you've got a four week sales cycle, at least you know about it a month ahead, because if you don't get any leads in, you don't make any sales. You might make sales this week, because you're converting leads that came in last month, but you won't make sales in four weeks time because your leads dropped off.

These are good examples of the sort of things that should be on your Scorecard because they put you in control. They give you visibility of the numbers that matter in your business.

If you set up your Scorecard properly, everything will have a goal and target.

So you'll have a target for 'Eye Tests This Week' and the number will either be green *(if it's on or ahead of target)* or red if it's off target each week. Now you can see in an instant, based on colour, how your business is doing.

And when you have those rolling 13 weeks, the picture becomes crystal clear.

The Score

Scorecard Template

	Week ending Jan 24	Week ending Jan 31	Week ending Feb 7	Week ending Feb 14	Week ending Feb 21	Week ending Feb 28	Week ending Mar 6	Week ending Mar 13	Week ending Mar 20	Week ending Mar 27

You won't get your Scorecard completely right from the very beginning. With every business we work with there are always iterations needed, and that's OK.

You learn, and it develops, as you go.

But the important thing is to start.

Quality not Quantity

The trick with your Scorecard is to hone in on the relatively small amount of numbers that really matter. If you find yourself tracking fifteen numbers, you've probably over-cooked it.

Less is normally more when it comes to your Scorecard.

It's much easier, and more impactful, for you, and your team, to get focused on four of five numbers than nineteen or twenty. Please remember that.

This is often one of the areas where business owners most need help when we are coaching them. Their instincts are to capture and track everything when, in truth, a small handful of numbers can paint 95% of the picture.

Examples of good numbers to track in your Scorecard might include:

- How many new enquiries came in this week?
- How many proposals were sent out?
- How many new customers came on board?
- Meeting conversion rate?
- How many new reviews did you get this week on the sites that matter?

- What's your accounts receivable balance as of Friday night?
- What's your accounts payable balance as of Friday night?

You get the picture. These are just examples. Your job is to identify the handful of measures that will tell you – and your team – that you're on track, or off track.

The rolling 13 weeks are really important, because they show you the 'direction of travel'. The trend and where it's going.

With a rolling 13 weeks, your Scorecard is not just a snapshot in time, but a living breathing manifestation of where things are heading. It means you can see at a glance whether things are getting better, getting worse, or moving in the right direction?
Both the Marketing Tracker and the Scorecard are really very straightforward to implement, once you're thinking clearly and accurately about your business.

The only challenging part is identifying what are the things that you want to track.

If you get into double figures, be very careful. In most businesses, your Scorecard can be kept to single figures in terms of the measures that you're tracking.

It's just a pulse. It's not a complete health scan.

It's designed to tell you enough so you know that the right things are happening.

And with these two elements in place you start to sleep better at night. All the uncertainty disappears.

Now, you know what's happening.

Now, you've got a proper grasp on the things that are important.

The Tracker and the Scorecard force you to get out of the weeds and focus on the things that matter to get you to where you want to be.

Now, you can move your business forward, because now you're in control.

There's a simple system of the right measures that will get you to where you need to get be.

CHAPTER SIXTEEN:

THE OPTIMISATION

"World domination is such an ugly phrase.

I prefer to call it world optimisation"

Eliezer Yudkowsky

The final part of the Entrepreneurs Marketing and Sales System isn't really a part at all.

You see, what we've discovered, over many years, is that the work to market a business properly is never really finished.

Similarly, the work to move a business owner up the money pyramid is never really complete either.

You have to keep working at this.

And the best way to think about it is in three cycles.

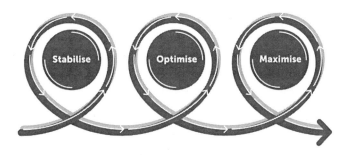

The first time you go through the System you are stabilising.

You're putting everything in place and getting a grip on the right things so you can properly take control of your business.

It typically takes 9 – 12 months to get every part of the System properly in place and stabilised. You know where and how it all fits together and where you're heading.

The Optimisation

At the end of stabilisation, you have customers coming in rhythmically, predictably, and consistently. You'll be servicing those customers competently and consistently. Operationally, you'll be solid.

Once it is *(stabilised)* you go through everything again, systematically, and you optimise.

Optimisation is the second cycle.

You make it better. You improve. You polish and tweak.

In the optimisation cycle, you'll start to improve things like your customer journey.

You'll start to remove yourself as a business owner from the sales process (because it's always going to be a big cap on your growth if you're the only one that can sell).

You also start to reduce your cost per acquisition, because you get better at the marketing based on the data that you have that's coming in. So, you optimise your different marketing funnels based on the activity and the results of what's happening.

Then, at the end of your optimisation phase, some businesses will go round again, this time in maximise mode.

Maximise mode is when you can properly hit the gas and start to expand into new markets.

You can introduce new products.

You might expand into new services.

All sorts of things can happen in maximise mode.

However you play it, the reality is that your Marketing System will always need maintaining.

Implementation will never be completely finished.

While we know that this System can deliver sustainable results in a matter of days, we also know that it takes a lifetime to master.

The benefits though can be life-changing, as they already have been for so many.

CHAPTER SEVENTEEN:
THE SUPPORT

"Anything is possible when you have the right people to support you..."

First of all, thank you for reading my book. But now you're at the final chapter, we've come to a fork in the road.

This can be the end, or a beginning.

If you've found this book interesting and useful, then I've got good news for you. There's plenty more where that came from.

Over the past decade my team and I spend our time helping tens of thousands of entrepreneurs to get and keep more customers and grow their businesses through Entrepreneurs Circle.

We're the UK's largest membership organisation dedicated to helping small businesses to grow and our hustling, bustling community of like minded business owners is the secret sauce behind literally thousands of hugely successful businesses here in the UK and abroad.

If you got a lot from the Entrepreneurs Marketing & Sales System - I can tell you you'll get infinitely more through the full Entrepreneurs Circle experience.

Tools, training, coaching and support to help you get more customers and bridge the gap between where your business is now and where you want it to be.

The impact we have on our members is remarkable - life changing...

And that's why, I'm offering you a gift.

Join Entrepreneurs Circle completely FREE, with no obligation whatsoever.

Head over to: **https://EntrepreneursCircle.org/BookOffer**

And see for yourself the impact EC can have on your business.

Join us for free. Let us help you implement the Entrepreneurs Marketing & Sales System in your business and finally crack the rhythmic acquisition of customers for good.

I sincerely hope that you make the right choice at this fork in the road, but whatever you decide, I wish you well on your business journey.

Thanks for reading,

P.S. On the next few pages you can see what business owners just like you have to say about Entrepreneurs Circle.

We have literally hundreds and hundreds of success stories, case studies and reviews on our website but here are a few of my favourites...

To see the full library of success stories from Entrepreneurs Circle Members, go to the page below *(warning: the page is 3 miles long!)* **https://EntrepreneursCircle.org/member-stories**

"I now have money in the bank"

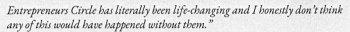

"Thanks to the EC team, I no longer have to look at the bank account every day and wonder how I'm going to pay the next bill because I've got money in the bank, which I never did before.

Entrepreneurs Circle has literally been life-changing and I honestly don't think any of this would have happened without them."

PAUL ETHERIDGE Run Hard Eat Cake

"We've grown by over £150,000"

"Turnover up. Margins up. Profits up. We've grown by over £150,000 thanks to Nigel and the team. To top it off, we've just moved into our dream home too!"

MARK POWELL MPD Creative

"The best business decision you'll ever make"

"Joining Entrepreneurs Circle was a big decision for me. Funds were low and my business was failing, but I can now say it was the best decision I've ever made!

It's transformed the way I think, the way I work and the way I run my business.

Our numbers are up big time year on year and it wouldn't have happened without Entrepreneurs Circle.

It really, really works!"

JAYNE REES Eve's Toy Shop
Winner of the Best Independent Toy Shop in the UK

"It keeps you on track – it's worth its weight in gold"

"It's easy to procrastinate when you're working on your own, but the EC team have kept me bang on track!

Just to know that every day, whatever issues you're facing, there is someone you can talk to and get help, advice, ideas — whatever you need — it's worth its weight in gold."

SANDRA LAWTON National Dog Training Academy

"We made an extra £15,000 from one call"

"A few months after joining Entrepreneurs Circle we've made an additional £15,000 exclusively because of their advice.

Without a doubt joining EC is the best thing we've ever done for our business.

Getting help, advice and coaching from Nige's team, people who've been there and done it — it's great!"

ALEX YOUNG Stanley Villa Farm

"I'm actually achieving my goals"

"I can't tell you how grateful I am for what the EC has done for me!

For the first time ever I'm actually making real progress and achieving my goals.

It's helped me become more focused and driven, and it's all thanks to Entrepreneurs Circle.

The accountability has been really helpful and I've hit every milestone so far."

JAMES FEAKES Java Cleaning

"I've been blown away by the practical help I've had."

"When I signed up to the Entrepreneurs Circle my business was in massive debt, my marriage was in tatters and I'll be honest, I signed up not expecting much.

18 months on and everything is so different.

Aside from everything that I've learned, I've been blown away by the practical help I've had. The utter sense of relief knowing that I wasn't alone in my position and that there were an entire hoard of people that were or have been suffering in the same way.

It has changed every aspect of my life. In August I took my family to Florida!! Never, ever would I have thought it was possible! We've booked to go again next year and we're going to Italy in April as well for good measure.

We're making decent money and I can see a bright future. That is really down to Entrepreneurs Circle"

BRENDAN O'NEILL Midlands Music Services Ltd

"We've doubled our profits in 12 months...!"

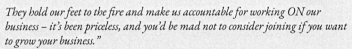

"The EC has transformed the way we run our business.

We've implemented some strategies that we would never have thought of ourselves and the results have been great.

They hold our feet to the fire and make us accountable for working ON our business – it's been priceless, and you'd be mad not to consider joining if you want to grow your business."

JAMES MIDDLEWICH Digital Group Media

"I've doubled my profits..."

"I've doubled my profits over the past year. I've been able to take my family to Disney in Florida (twice!) and buy my dream car – all thanks to the EC..."

DEREK MASON Super Structure Associates

"From my worst year to my best year in 12 months thanks to the EC"

After having had my worst ever year in business last year I was really sceptical about joining the EC – but I'm so glad I did.

It's made a huge difference to my business and with four months to go I already know that this will be my best year in business – so quite a turnaround.

I have NEVER sold this many wedding dresses in the first 7 months of the year!!!

So pleased I took the plunge."

ANNA HARE Pure Brides

"I'm killing my financial targets now…"

"Before joining the EC in 2018, I felt I was just going around in circles with my business and my ideas - it was like being on a hamster wheel.

I knew I was awesome at what I do but I was just getting more and more tangled up working IN my business not ON it.

I didn't know where to turn for the right help and advice then thankfully I met the EC and everything has changed since.

I finally learnt the right way to think about my business, my planning, my processes and my systems, goals and targets.

I'm killing my financial targets now and on average our sales are up almost 80% every month, year-on-year, which has made such a massive difference.

OMG, I'm in tears writing this...

...THANK YOU, THANK YOU, THANK YOU AND THANK YOU,

BECAUSE JUST LIKE THE SONG....I CAN SEE CLEARLY NOW THE RAIN HAS GONE!!!

I've been through so much in the last few years but now things are properly under control."

MAXINE RODRIGUEZ The Pain Physio

You can download all of the tools referenced in this book at
EMSSystem.co.uk/downloads